INTIMATE GLIMPSES OF MYSTERIOUS TIBET AND NEIGHBOURING COUNTRIES

Sincerely,
E. O. Knight.

INTIMATE GLIMPSES
OF
MYSTERIOUS TIBET
AND
NEIGHBOURING COUNTRIES

G.E.O. KNIGHT

GYAN

Published by

Gyan Publishing House
5, Ansari Road
Daryaganj, New Delhi-110002
Phone: 011-47034999, 9811692060
E-mail: books@gyanbooks.com

Distribution Network
gyanbooks.com
India, USA, Canada, UK, Australia, France

ISBN : 978-81-212-3629-4 (PB)
First Published, London, 1930

2nd Impression 2020

Printed at: Gyan Press, Delhi.

Intimate Glimpses of Mysterious Tibet
and
Neighbouring Countries
Author: G.E.O. Knight

INTIMATE GLIMPSES OF MYSTERIOUS TIBET AND NEIGHBOURING COUNTRIES

G. E. O. KNIGHT, F.R.G.S.

Corresponding Member, Royal Botanic Society of London, etc., etc.,

Leader, British Expedition to Tibet (1922-3).

LONDON:
THE GOLDEN VISTA PRESS
(ANGLO-AMERICAN PUBLICATIONS),
FETTER HOUSE,
FETTER LANE, E.C.4.
1930.

FOREWORD.

In the following pages, I have endeavoured to present a faithful sketch of a series of travels made by me in such truly romantic countries as Tibet, Sikkim, Nepal, etc. It is needless perhaps to say that this little book has not been written for the scholar, but solely for those jaded men and women who love reading stories of adventure and of distant lands. To all such I commend the work for what it is worth.

G. E. O. KNIGHT.

London, W.2.
1930.

INTRODUCTION.

THE ORIGIN OF THE TIBETAN EXPEDITION.

Our journey to Tibet was due to a very small incident, odd as the story may seem. A casual ride on a 'bus in London in 1921 not only culminated in one of the biggest and most daring adventures in Tibet, but it was also instrumental in introducing to the notice of the British and American publics the first moving pictures of the City of the Undying Dalai Lama that lies in the very heart of the great Asiatic continent.

A lecturing engagement had taken us to Bloomsbury. The night was damp and foggy, so we occupied a seat inside the 'bus. A discarded copy of a trade journal caught our eye, and quite casually we turned over its leaves. In a rather obscure corner of the publication was a paragraph that ran to this effect: "What a splendid opportunity now exists for securing the first motion pictures of Lhasa, the Forbidden City of Tibet!" From that moment the idea haunted us, and we set about thinking very hard, a thing we are quite unaccustomed to do. As the days passed, the determination to be the first to secure possession of the trophy grew stronger and stronger, and though the struggle was a hard one, we never lost sight of the ideal.

It is perfectly true that many years previous to this incident, we had been interested in Tibet and Tibetan lore. It was Sven Hedin who first brought the country to our notice. In our hot youth, we had determined to visit the "Roof of the World," come what may. Our joy may be imagined when at long last we saw an opportunity of going to the Forbidden Land with a definite object in view. Not for a moment did we stop to consider the many political and physical obstacles that stood in the way of achieving our object. These did not trouble us in the least. Other men had got into the country, and what other men had done, we too were able to do. What concerned us at the time was how to convince business men of the soundness of a business proposition. It took us more than fifteen months before we succeeded in securing the necessary funds for the Expedition. Having done this, our next step was to secure the permission of the India Office in London to proceed as far as Gyantse, one of the British Trading stations in the interior of the Forbidden Land. On the understanding that we were not to proceed farther than Gyantse without the consent of the Indian and the Tibetan Governments, the permission was eventually forthcoming.

In this manner, five male Europeans set out for the "Roof of the World," to the accompaniment of questions in the House of Commons as to the *military* nature of the Expedition, and the jeers and chuckles of the London and provincial Press, who one and all declared that the task the Expedition had set itself was impossible of realisation.

But the *impossible* has ever appealed to us. As Leader of the Expedition, we had determined upon our own course of action before leaving London for the East. If the Governments of India and Tibet refused to grant us permission to proceed to Lhasa in a gentlemanly way, there was an alternative course of action. As events afterward turned out, we were asked by the Indian Government to leave the country after a fruitless application had been made by us to visit Lhasa. To quote the telegram handed to us by the Tibetan Trade Agent in Gyantse, on behalf of the Political Officer in Gantok:—

"*Substance of a telegram dated Lhasa, 28th October,* 1922, *from the Prime Minister of Tibet to the Political Officer in Gantok.*

"*With regard to the request of Mr. G. E. O. Knight and his friends asking permission to proceed to Lhasa, we consulted the National Assembly in the matter. They say . . . . that they fear other foreigners may ask for permission to come to Lhasa . . . . The National Assembly, after much consideration, has decided to send a letter to the Tibetan Trade Agent to explain matters, and to request the Mission to return the same way as they came. We hope they will not misunderstand our action in refusing permission . . . . We will always appreciate interest taken in our country. We sincerely hope Mr. Knight will understand our difficulties, and will not be disappointed and go away with ill-feeling in his heart. We have to be very careful not to hurt the feelings of our own people, even though we wish to be kind to our friends. We wish the Mission a safe return and success in their future researches."*

On the receipt of the letter referred to in the telegram (a wonderful piece of "facing both ways" document) and so unlike the generous impulses governing the telegram just quoted, we deemed it expedient and gentlemanly to quit Gyantse for our base at Darjeeling, and make an assault on Lhasa without the knowledge or permission of the Indian and Tibetan Governments. That story has been partially written by the Scientific Adviser of the Expedition, Dr. W. M. McGovern, and it is here unnecessary to say more than that the Author of that remarkable book came to us when our own plans for undertaking the journey were well advanced, and that we relinquished them in favour of our learned friend solely because we deemed him to be the fitter man for the work.

DARJEELING.

The blue sky is the temple's arch,
Its transept Earth and Air,
The music of its starry march,
The chorus of a prayer.
The mists above the morning rills
Rise white as the wings of prayer;
The altar curtains of the hills,
Are sunset's purple air.

Whittier.

The journey from Calcutta to Darjeeling is a never-to-be-forgotten undertaking. The first stage, across the lower Gangetic plain, is through a most uninteresting country from the scenic point of view—just an interminable plain of jute and rice fields with occasional palm and bamboo trees to break the monotony of the vista. The River Ganges, the sacred river of the Hindus, is spanned by the Hardinge Bridge a few hours after leaving the commercial capital of India. This bridge is considered one of the finest engineering feats in the world. Two and a half million cubic feet of water pass under it every second at high flood. The guide banks therefore had to be constructed to protect the bridge from the assaults of the waters below.

It is not until the traveller reaches Siliguri, however, some twelve hours' run from Calcutta, that he obtains a first view of the great snowy peaks of the Eastern Himalaya. At Siliguri the terminus of the Eastern Bengal Railway is reached, and the starting point of the Darjeeling Himalayan Railway.

On account of the unique contour of the mountains, the curves of the Darjeeling Himalayan Railway are very sharp, no tunnels being bored. There is one curve which has a radius of fifty-nine feet! The total mileage from Siliguri to Darjeeling is only fifty-one miles, but a perpendicular height of 1½ miles has to be attained before Darjeeling is reached. It takes about 7½ hours to reach the hill station from Siliguri, or approximately twenty-one hours from Calcutta.

A few minutes after leaving Siliguri, the little train crosses the Mahanaddi Bridge over the river of that name. Then a comparatively level track is traversed until Sukna Station is reached, and it is in the neighbourhood of this station that the ground *suddenly* rises. The traveller is now at the foothills of the mighty Himalaya. The mountain ranges appear more and more numerous as the ascent to Darjeeling is made, the first tea gardens are seen as the traveller leaves Sukna behind, lofty forest trees, giving out a sweet but pungent smell, begin to line the route. The track up a spur of the Singalela range on which Darjeeling is situated, is thrown off by the second highest mountain in the world, Mount Kanchenjunga,* itself the centre of a group, of which Jannu, Great Kabru, and Pandim are the next highest, in the order given. The loftiest peaks, it is interesting to note, are outside British territory.

The journey to Darjeeling passes through the finest sal and toon forests extant. Wild elephants, tigers, leopards, buffaloes, wolves, and other creatures of the forests have been known to dispute the peaceful passage of the little train that hisses its way through magnificent forests to its destination. The foliage is remarkable for its variety and beauty. Creepers pendant from the lofty trees, bamboo grass in abundance everywhere the eye travels, tea plantations to right and left, and spick and span bungalows of the planters, form a charming feature of the surroundings. The incline becomes more steep, the track winds about that is both bewildering and amazing. The engine never seems to run a straight course, at one moment it is to the right of the observer, at another to the left. Onwards and upwards we go. The track is often seen hundreds of feet below the train, and one wonders how on earth one has got from

* It is either Kanchenjunga or K, of the Karakoram that is the second highest mountain in the world. The question is still in dispute.

that point to this. A luxuriance of ever-changing vegetation greets the eye everywhere, and from time to time it is even possible to get a glimpse of the heated and barren plains of Bengal, several thousands of feet below the observer. Picturesque hill people are now seen, people with strong Mongoloid countenances. The countryside is observed to be dotted here and there with tall bamboo poles with strips of linen attached, these are the prayer flags of Lamaism. From the heat of the plains the traveller will have noted that at 5,000 feet elevation he is approaching a temperate climate, and the vegetation has changed from tropical to sub-tropical varieties. The brownish-grey of the oak, the rich green of the laurels, and the wondrous waxlike beauty of the magnolias and carmine of rhododendrons —these have taken the place of tropical foliage.

As Ghum, the highest point of the Darjeeling-Himalayan Railway is approached, the Abode of Snow, as the Himalaya is so aptly named, now stand out in their mantle of purity against the azure blue of the sky, changing at sunset to pale pink, then as the light wanes to deep crimson, till the great gold sun dies down, leaving them dead white against the background of purple clouds around.

The town of Darjeeling is ideally situated. It stands on the crest of a long ridge that has its origin in Kanchenjunga, visible from Darjeeling on any clear day as the most conspicuous of the many peaks that flank this eminence. The immensity and extent of the Eastern Himalaya as seen from the hill station makes the panorama one of the most wonderful in the whole world, and the town's fame is due, in large measure, to the magnificence of the spectacle spread out before the observer in glittering array.

When lit up by the rays of the rising or the setting sun, the "Abode of Snow" is seen to its greatest advantage. The tints defy description. Dr. Hooker, who knew the Himalaya better than many men living to-day, has furnished a wonderful description of the sublime sight. *Inter alia*, he wrote: "The firmament appeared of a pale steel blue, and a broad low arch spanned the horizon, bounded by a line of the little fleecy clouds; below this the sky was of a golden yellow, while in successively deeper strata, many belts or ribbons of vapour appeared to press upon the plains, the lowest of which was of a dark leaden hue, the upper more purple, and vanishing into the pale yellow above. Gradually the golden lines grew dim, and the blues and purples gained depth of colour; till the sun set behind the dark blue-peaked mountains in a flood of crimson and purple, sending broad beams of grey shade and purple light up to the zenith and all around. As evening advanced, mists rapidly formed below me in little isolated spots, which coalesced and spread out like a heaving sea, leaving nothing above their surface but the ridges and spurs of the adjacent mountains . . . . As darkness came on, and the stars arose, a light fog gathered around me, and I quitted with reluctance one of the most impressive and magic scenes I had ever beheld."

One of the best views of the eternal snows is to be got from Tiger Hill, on the summit of Senchal Mountain, 8,515 feet up and distant some 4½ miles from Darjeeling itself. The altitude of Darjeeling is just under 7,000 feet, with a very humid climate. It is probably the dampest region in the whole of the Himalaya, with a mean temperature for the whole year of 56° F., the difference between the hottest and the coldest months being one of 22° F. only, with a mean barometric pressure of twenty-three inches. The effects on the human body owing to the difference in atmospheric pressure at sea level and high altitudes are interesting. At sea level, the ordinary man is pressed upon by a weight of 30,000 lbs. At Darjeeling the load is reduced to one of 22,500 lbs., with no injurious effects on the human body. The visitor finds himself a little short of breath at first, and occasionally complains of headache, and he may experience a sense of sickness. But all these sensations disappear after a few days' stay in the town, and people go about their work and pleasure without suffering much inconvenience.

It is in the higher altitudes that vertigo and mountain

air sickness begin to make themselves manifest. There is little doubt that every man and woman has his and her maximum altitude, beyond which further going is impossible. We have been up to 20,000 feet in Tibet, and no doubt could have gone beyond had time and circumstances permitted. It is curious how the effects of altitude differ with the same individual on different days. Once at 17,550 feet we thought we could not proceed another foot. On the next day we suffered little or no inconvenience in attaining the 20,000 feet altitude. Lassitude and tension in fact were greater at the lower elevation. Irritability was a noticeable feature among us.

During the monsoon, Darjeeling is a town of fogs and mists. The annual rainfall is very heavy, one hundred and fourteen inches on the average. October, November, and December are the dryest months of the year. During the wet season, it is impossible to keep anything dry in the house. You go to bed in damp pyjamas, sleep in damp sheets and blankets, lie on a damp mattress, and hear the drip, drip, drip of water from the walls throughout the night.

Few towns in the world contain a more polyglot population than Darjeeling, where the hill tribes from around and the peoples from the plains congregate in bewildering array. Among these are the Bhutias, Bengalis, Tibetans, Nepalese, Lepchas, Sherpas, Bhutanese, Mechis, and a host of others dressed in their characteristic, highly coloured costumes that almost distinguishes each from the other. Most of them are of Mongolian type and of Tibetan extraction. Generally speaking, the men are of a sturdy type, happy-go-lucky, inveterate gamblers, and embrace one of the two schools of Tibetan Lamaism. The women are also of fine physique, have dirty yellow complexions and paint their faces as do women all the world over. They load their necks with heavy ornaments of cheap jewellery, wear anklets and armlets of turquoise and jade, short blouses and highly coloured skirts, and like their men folk, they are a boisterous and care-free lot. Nothing seems to trouble them very much. It is seldom that one sees the women doing nothing, but the men sit about when not working, whiling away the fleeting moments either in gambling or smoking, and Micawber-like, wait for something to turn up. When at work, they are apparently tireless, and can perform an amazing amount of hard labour. They make excellent servants on the whole. If one is engaged as a cook, he will deduct a certain percentage from the housekeeping money for his own use. If you demur, he will leave your service, and argue that it is the custom in all parts of India for "cookie" to enjoy the privilege of stealing as much as he possibly can from his mistress's household expenses. His business is to cook, and not to discuss moral questions.

The man who sits at the entrance to the cave at the foot of Observatory Hill in Darjeeling is worth a passing notice. When we first met him, we were disposed to be impressed by his wisdom and learning, when we left him, we were certain that we lacked knowledge of our fellow creatures. He described himself as a yogin, that is, one who has achieved his yoga, over whom nothing perishable has any more power. He told us he wanted to pray for our "prosperity," and was candid enough to say we looked in need of salvation. But he never prayed for anyone without a cash payment in advance. The more that was given him, the longer would be the prayer, and presumably the more efficacious it would prove to be. We do not like people praying for us, and we never pray for ourselves or for others. We have never prayed for ourselves, in fact, for we have never had anything to pray for. A few rupees, we were told, would bring us in close association with Krishna. We have never had any desire to get into association with Krishna, although we did not so say to the yogin. We enquired how many rupees were necessary, and were informed that five would be ample. We offered two as a deposit. We were told it would be necessary for us to penetrate far, far into the cave, alone and unaccompanied by man or beast. At a given point, we were to indulge in deep meditation. The cave, we were assured, led to Lhasa, Kanchenjunga, and Benares, all holy places. We have a great dislike for holy places and always avoid them, if possible. Some years ago a fellow creature offered to take us to Mecca, but we declined. We would have gone to the North Pole with him, but to Mecca—no. Not for all the gold in the world. We penetrated as far as the cave in Darjeeling would allow, about one-sixteenth of an English mile. Do not for a moment imagine, dear reader, that we believed it led to Lhasa, Kanchenjunga, and Benares, some 400, 36 and 300 miles distant respectively, as the crow flies. That is the reason why we only paid two rupees. We paused as directed, and meditated on man's deceit in general. Nothing happened to us save that we bumped our head against the stone wall, and some icy water trickled down our back. We uttered a mild form of oath, and that would probably keep Krishna coming near us. We strolled leisurely back, and reprimanded the yogin for his deceit. It would seem, however, that the fault was ours, so we had to apologise. The cave, we were assured, did lead to the holy places in question in the spiritual, and in no other sense of the expression. But we did not pay any more rupees, preferring to settle any difference with our friend in our next incarnation.

One of the most interesting races to be found in Darjeeling is the Lepcha, reputed to speak the oldest language in the world. The Lepchas are the aborigines of Sikkim, and are believed to have once possessed the whole of the hill country of what is now known as Independent Sikkim and British Darjeeling. Later, the Tibetans arrived and dispossessed them of their heritage, and to-day they are a conquered people, living in the main under British rule.

The Lepchas have a tradition of a man and woman survivors of a flood that overwhelmed their country. The Lepcha man and woman are popularly believed to have reached the summit of Mount Tendong, 8,000 feet above sea level, from which they began replenishing the earth. In Darjeeling, Mount Tendong is sometimes called Mount Ararat, owing, it is said, to a similarity in contour between it and the pretty illustrations of

Ararat found in children's coloured picture books. It is interesting to note that Mount Tendong is in proximity to a very famous river, a great spur from Kanchenjunga terminating in Tendong, and butting in between the Great Rungeet and the Tambur Rivers. In all probability there were overflowings in times past that may account for the Lepcha " universal " deluge.

The Lepcha race is remarkable in several particulars. It has been estimated that there are about six thousand Lepchas living in Sikkim alone. The geographical distribution of the race affords some peculiar features. As a general rule, the Lepchas live in scattered groups and not in communities. They not only dwell in Sikkim, but are to be found in the Darjeeling district, Bhutan, and adjacent lands. One of their favourite habits is to emigrate, and little Bhutan has many hundreds of Lepchas within her territory to-day. This latter country offers them facilities that are not met with elsewhere in this part of the world.

The Lepcha race is one of the least prolific, and its studied indifference to family and communal life is remarkable. There is little or no cohesion among them. Generally speaking, they are timid and peaceful, and happy most when in their beloved forests. They have long since been ousted by the enterprising Nepalese in every walk of life. They are born naturalists, and birds and animals seldom flee from them. They have their own name for every plant and animal. Most of them are Animists, with a sprinkling of Buddhism and Lamaism among them. They never kill for what the White Man calls " the love of sport." In Darjeeling there are many mongrel races directly linked with the Lepchas—crosses between them and the Tibetans, Sherpas, etc.

Here is a rough translation of a Lepcha poem, the first of its kind that has ever been published. We should here say that we know nothing of the Lepcha language. The general idea of the poem was communicated to us through an interpreter. We have called it, " The Soul of the Lepcha."

To the green fresh leaves I spoke,
To the pine and to the oak,
To the flowers that strew the ground,
To the moss that gathers round.
To the far and to the nigh,
To the blue and radiant sky.
To the insects sporting here,
To the water running there.
To the meadow, to the hill,
To the lively and the still,
To one and all the things I love,
On Mother Earth, in skies above.

As soon as the traveller ascends the hills from Siliguri, he comes face to face with a population wholly different in appearance and customs from the peoples of the plains of Bengal. The differences indeed are so obvious that they strike even the casual observer at once. The Mongolian type of countenance, with hair uniformly black, skin a dirty yellowish brown, slightly prognathous jaws, high and prominent cheek bones, small, black and oblique eyes, are met with on the road to Darjeeling and beyond. Men and women of the Mongolian races become more numerous as the confines of Darjeeling are reached.

In the Darjeeling Terai, or sub-montane strip of territory covered with stunted and bushy timber, live the Mechis, an inoffensive, industrious people who exist by cultivating cleared forests, and by the sale of jungle products. Like the Lepchas, they are nomadic in their habits, seldom staying in any one place beyond a year. A peculiarity of the Mechis is that they thrive only in malarial districts. If they are transported to districts where the anopheles mosquito is absent, they succumb almost immediately to the ravages of pneumonia! Each family manufactures its own furniture and builds its own house, makes its own garments, cultivates its own ground and, generally speaking, fends for itself. The women weave and spin and wash the family garments, they wear gold and silver rings in their noses and ears, and bracelets adorn their wrists and feet. They are a very hospitable race, generally speaking. Their religion consists in the worship of sun, moon, and stars, wind, rain, storms, and rivers. In marriage the bride has to be purchased, but there are no child marriages among them, marriage taking place when they are adults. One of the features of the marriage ceremony is the sacrifice of a cock and hen, the bridegroom holding the former and the bride the latter. The officiating priest severs the heads of both birds at the same moment and the direction in which the blood flows serves as a guide as to the happiness or otherwise of the union.

The Limboes formerly ruled over a part of Nepal, but were driven out by the Gurkhas, or Nepalese. They are a very brave and cruel race, and many of them are to be found in Indian regiments. Their customs are not dissimilar to those of the Mechis. In religion they are Animists, and they practice polyandry. The language of the Limboes has no written characters.

The most conspicuous and numerous of the aboriginal tribes of Darjeeling is the Bhutia. They are of several classes, but all make good servants, doing most of the dirty work of the day. Generally speaking, they are not given to washing themselves, but they are strong and industrious, and as a rule, are fairly honest. It is seldom that one is not struck by their good humour and happy-go-lucky dispositions. Gambling and drunkenness are inherent in them, polyandry a recognised institution among them. Modesty is not one of their strong features. Their religion is the Red School of Lamaism, they believe in the efficacy of the Prayer Wheel and the Prayer Flag.

Within recent years, the Nepalese have over-run Darjeeling. They now form 75 per cent. of the population of the hill station. They are a very enterprising race, make good colonists, and are famous as agriculturists, carpenters, blacksmiths, domestic servants, etc. In physique, they are wiry, agile, short and slim, very active and brave.

In Darjeeling there is a patois known as "The Language of the Gods." It is used in all official police records!

SIKKIM.

The small independent State of Sikkim, the most northerly outpost of the Indian Empire, buffeted between Nepal and Bhutan, is not only a land of gigantic forests, mighty mountains, precipitous hills, picturesque dales, and lovely valleys, but also of wild, open spaces where enormous glaciers carve out the surface of the land, and where the second highest mountain in the world rears its head some 28,146 feet a few miles outside of Sikkimese territory.

Sikkim is a land of contrasts. One may pass through a country containing a steamy atmosphere to one of piercing winds and fierce snowstorms, and their intermediate stages. In the hot districts, insect life is found in abundance, and every shade of colour abounds. Bamboo trees, ferns, lichens, moss and orchids greet the astonished eye in every direction. A veritable sea of loveliness covers the major portion of the land. The approach to the frozen north is through a country laden with treacherous forests over ground of black mud and slime, infested with leeches, tree ticks, and stinging plants, through well-nigh impassable barriers in the form of huge boulders that necessitate lengthy détours, in an atmosphere of moisture that penetrates every particle of clothing, making life almost unbearable. There are ascents and descents varying 4,000 to 18,000 feet above sea level, through overgrown paths thick with vegetable matter in an advanced stage of decomposition. Obstacles too numerous to mention meet the jaded traveller at almost every turn in his quest of the outer ridges of the Eastern Himalaya, and when at last he finds himself at the foot of these eminences, his troubles are by no means ended. But he has attained practically virgin soil. Mount Kanchenjunga, part of whose base lies within Sikkimese territory, has never yet been ascended, nor have any of the lesser mountains in its immediate neighbourhood. Few white men have been privileged to travel in the neighbourhood of these striking objects, which, as viewed from any vantage point, not alone charm the sight but overawe the imagination.

The journey to Sikkim from Darjeeling is accomplished over a number of very deep, heavily forested valleys. Curiously enough, these valleys run almost parallel to one another, necessitating a series of ascents and descents that changes one's elevation from minute to minute. There are falls and rises of several thousands of feet, but in approaching Tibet the ascents are greater than the descents. Level going is unknown in the vicinity of the Himalaya. This up and down mode of travelling is very fatiguing, both to man and beast. Most travellers are anxious to secure a view of the eternal snows at a higher altitude than Darjeeling. We caught our first good view of the Eastern Himalaya when we arrived at the Jelap La, 14,390 feet above sea level.

The journey from Darjeeling to the Tibetan frontier was done in easy stages. Our first trek was across the 28 miles to Kalimpong, where we had the pleasure of being shown something of the splendid work done by Dr. J. A. Graham and his co-workers. Christian Missionary enterprise in India has not proved the success once entertained of it, but Dr. Graham and his family have certainly accomplished miracles in Kalimpong and its neighbourhood. The town is some 6,400 feet up, and it was shrouded in dense mists on the afternoon of our arrival. The Dak Bungalow, a roomy and comfortable building, had been reserved for our reception by courtesy of the Indian Government.

Early the next morning, we left Kalimpong after a delay caused by a breakage to our cine-camera. It appeared that Anqui, one of our servants, had let fall the instrument on to the head of one of his associates while in a drunken brawl. We dropped by easy stages from 6,400 feet to the hamlet of Pedong at 4,800 feet, where we rested for the night. On the following day we found ourselves at Rhenok, a small village at some 3,300 feet up, and from thence we resumed our journey to Ari, 4,700 feet.

The next day brought us with another descent, the Rongli River at 2,600 feet. Here we met a Tibetan woman with almost Caucasian features—white skin, rosy cheeks, blue eyes, and golden hair. Later we learned that her type is quite a common feature of the country, particularly among the Dru-pas, peaceful, nomadic or semi-nomadic tribes, who live generally in tents on the northern plateaux of Tibet some 16,000 feet above sea level. It is highly probable that they have a Caucasian strain in them. It is possible to recognise a common racial stamp in the facial expression, etc., of the people, reminding one instinctively of Europeans. Several such we had occasion to meet at Gautsa on our way up the Roof of the World.

We rested at Rongli for two days. We had been warned that our next stage was a hard and treacherous one. And so it proved to be. From 2,600 feet we had to climb to Sedonchen, 6,600 feet above sea level. The going was bad. The terrific rains of the last few days had washed away the roads, and in addition brought down hundreds of boulders that now blocked our progress. The mules were worn out before we had accomplished one half of the journey. The bad weather added to our discomforts. Snow began to fall in places, riders and mules found themselves in an occasional bog, from which they had to be extricated. Once we were up to our necks in mud and slime. We not only looked, but felt a sorry party. Our commissariat suffered greatly, a considerable quantity of foodstuffs and clothing, together with a mule, disappeared over a precipice several thousands of feet beneath us, and we nearly lost our Transport Officer in much the same manner. But he was a Sergeant-Major, and just knew how to pull himself together and address his mule in terms that only Sergeant-Majors know how.

There are some people who insist that the mule is a contrary and wanton beast. That could not be said of the mules that formed so large a part of our transport. They took us up and along, and their patience and faithfulness was extraordinary. What we should have done without them we know not. They solved problems for us that we ourselves knew not how to solve. We soon found that if left to themselves, they negotiated the most difficult and treacherous paths alone, spurning our assistance and turning a deaf ear to every command we gave. That we were the asses and they but mules was manifest. Sometimes we objected to a too close approach to the sides of the precipice where a slip on the part of the beast would have hurled us to destruction. But they were always sure-footed. Sometimes they would playfully pretend to slip, but for the most they just ambled along, quite content with their humble lot in life.

It was our mules that eventually got us up to Sedonchen, not we ourselves. For this service, we gave them a couple of days' rest, and also an extra bag of corn. That they understood and appreciated the privilege was evident when the time came for us to part from them, and to take on a fresh relay of animals. To our surprise, they one and all waited on us as does a deputation to the Chancellor of the Exchequer, or another Minister of State. They flatly refused to return to Darjeeling with their owner and rambled round our camp instead. It was not before this incident took place that we realised what it means for mules to have their backs up against the wall. Naturally, we re-engaged them on the spot, and not until we had reached Phari, reputed to be the foulest place on God's earth, did our little friends mutiny and decide there and then to accompany their owner back to Darjeeling rather than sniff the air of Phari, the Foul.

Our next stopping place was Gnatong, 12,200 feet up, the highest point we had yet attained. Here we rested awhile and partook of our first taste of Tibetan tea, native made.

To the north of us lay the Tibetan passes. We were about to leave Sikkimese territory and enter the Forbidden Land over the Jelap La, 14,390 feet above sea level. Eight miles away, and a stiff climb at that, we saw the pass enveloped in fog and mist. We had over 2,000 feet ascent in front of us. Before proceeding, we gave instructions for the mules to be fed.

It was about ten in the morning when we left Gnatong, and two hours later we found ourselves on the summit of the Jelap La. A cairn of stones from which fluttered innumerable prayer flags was added to by each one of us, as becomes every visitor to Tibet. Suddenly the clouds lifted, and we caught our first glimpse of Tibet, the Mysterious. Ninety miles away as the crow flies stood out against all else the glittering cone of Mount Chumolhari. In the valley beneath was a frozen lake. The descent into the Chumbi Valley necessitated our negotiating what seemed to be a wall inclined some sixty degrees from the horizontal. It was quite impossible for us to ride down this, and it took the better part of an hour to drop some 4,400 feet into the valley beneath, which is itself some 10,000 feet above sea level.

But we were now in Tibet. There was no one to apologise to us for the waywardness of the roads, which are not really roads but obstacles to progress, like most things Tibetan, as we were very soon to learn.

THE CHUMBI VALLEY.

As soon as we reached Yatung, our first business was to pay a formal visit to the Tibetan Depön, the chief official of the beautiful Chumbi Valley. The Chumbi Valley, by the way, is unlike any other part of Tibet. It is a valley on the south side of the Eastern Himalaya, forming a sort of wedge between the two small countries of Sikkim and Bhutan. The valley is well wooded, the sides are covered with numerous overhanging trees, while the rainfall is not inconsiderable. Many beautiful bungalows of rich Chinese and Indian merchants are to be found here. Yatung is the "capital" of the valley.

The Depön's house we found to be a well-built and substantial looking building, in the centre of the usual courtyard. Its architecture was typically Chinese. The door of the house was painted in rich Chinese colours, bearing an astrological figure to which wonderful effects were ascribed.

Entering, we had to ascend to the second floor, where we were introduced to the Depön. The room was large and spotlessly clean, the walls hung with magnificent Chinese draperies, while the furniture was typical of the Flowery Land. The Depön we found to be a charming host, interested in politics and photography. He insisted on being photographed with his "illustrious" guests, promising in the meanwhile to make favourable representations to Lhasa on our behalf. He assured us that, since our arrival, the plains of Tibet were blooming with the lotus flower, and His Most Exalted Highness and Holiness, the Dalai Lama, was passing sleepless nights anxiously awaiting our arrival in the city of the gods! He flattered us for nearly ten minutes, after which he began to suspect that some of the things he was saying were not being readily absorbed by us. Later we learned that his despatches to Lhasa were not in our favour, that in fact he had taken a violent dislike to all of us. And small wonder! The Leader of the Expedition was dressed in airman's outfit, the Cinematographer was in plus fours, while the Transport Officer looked minus a pair of trousers in kilts. What the Depön thought, we hardly dare venture to guess. That he was not impressed was obvious. However, we felt grateful to him for his hospitality, for we were hungry after our march from Langram along a road that was strewn with boulders and rocks purposely placed there to prevent people passing unobserved into Tibet. We made the Depön and his charming wife a few presents, which we thought were appropriate. He said he was delighted with everything he got, and we left him with the impression that he expected much more from us.

Our next meeting was with the British Trade Agent, or Consul-General, in the person of Mr. David MacDonald, a personal friend of the Dalai Lama, and a man much respected in this part of the world. A great Tibetan scholar, Mr. MacDonald for some years acted as intermediary between the Tibetan and Indian Governments, and was the ideal man for the position. Mr. MacDonald told us much about Tibet, and promised to do his utmost on our behalf, which he certainly did.

A few hours after meeting Mr. MacDonald we were introduced to Col. F. M. Bailey, the Political Officer who had charge of diplomatic negotiations with Tibet and Bhutan. Col. Bailey makes a most charming host, is a gentleman of wide experience of the East, and succeeded Sir Charles Bell as Political Officer in Sikkim. Certain information had reached us, before meeting Col. Bailey, that in no circumstances should we be allowed to proceed to Lhasa. In spite of this, we were asked to sign a declaration that we should not proceed beyond Gyantse without the consent of the Indian and the Tibetan Governments. On several occasions it had been hinted to us by one of the highest officials in Gyantse that if we cared to make a secret journey to Lhasa without the authority of either Government, no troops or police would be sent to bring us back. When we pointed out to the official that we were under obligation to the Political Officer in Gantok not to deviate from the route allotted us, the Tibetan official was violently sarcastic about the Indian Government, and demanded to know on whose authority the Political Officer was acting, and for how long Tibet had been an integral part of the Indian Empire!

During our stay in Yatung, we were the guests of Mr. MacDonald, who happened at the time to be entertaining a well-known Brigand Chieftainess, a Bhutanese Amazon, who had three husbands and wanted a fourth. For diplomatic reasons, it often falls to the lot of Government officials to entertain people of doubtful reputation. What Mr. MacDonald thought of us, we do not know. It was the first time that Mr. MacDonald had entertained a party of Britishers whose avowed object was to secure the pioneer film of the City of Lhasa, which for "diplomatic" reasons was not looked upon with favour by the Indian Government. But Governments are powerless against private enterprise and determination. We were determined to get the film, come what may, by fair means or foul. The film was got after fruitless negotiations with the Tibetan and Indian Governments.

The Bhutanese Chieftainess, it appears, had been plundering frontier peoples, and the Indian Government had been requested to put a stop to these malpractices. So the Chieftainess came to parley with the authorities. It was our privilege to meet the lady and her husbands. She was certainly a very strapping woman, courageous no doubt, with nice bobbed hair, but very much afraid of dogs. Her husbands she treated with the greatest contempt. All three certainly looked very lame and tame ducks. The while she was with us, she cast longing eyes on our Cinematographer. A dog happened to bark in front of her. With a shriek she bounded forward, and fell into the arms of the surprised cameraman. Did the husbands rush forward and help their spouse? Not a bit of it. They went on chewing betel. After that experience, the Leader of the Expedition deemed it prudent to keep his eyes on the Cinematographer, for he hourly expected to hear of his being kidnapped and added to the harem of the Chieftainess.

We were sorry to leave the beautiful Chumbi Valley. Our reception had been of the friendliest. We shall never forget the games of tennis we played there, 10,000 feet above sea level, and the football matches we had, to say nothing of our Bridge parties and dinners in the Dak Bungalow. The dinner we gave in honour of Col. and the Hon. Mrs. Bailey and Lady Cozens Hardy was a remarkable affair. We had to convert a small bedroom into a dining room. How we managed it, we hardly know, yet the table looked as neat as any in the Savoy Hotel, for instance, on a gala night.

TIBET.

Tibet suffers from too many labels. It is known as "The Forbidden Land," "The Land of Mountains, Monasteries, and Monks," "The Hermit Kingdom," "The Land of Women, Dogs and Dirt," "The Country of the Great Unwashed," "The Roof of the World," etc., each more or less descriptive of the land. But it was not until we had actually set foot on the soil of the Dalai Lama's dominions that we realised the significance of each of these labels. We were forbidden by the Indian Government to deviate as much as a mile from the route mapped out for us; we found ourselves face to face with mountains, monasteries and monks; we learned that hundreds of men had withdrawn from the world altogether and were either living in caves or in cells in the numerous monasteries scattered over the length and breadth of the country; we came in contact with women, dogs and dirt everywhere we went; we saw that the Tibetans, generally speaking, were in dire need of soap and water, while the difficulty of breathing and going about in our customary manner convinced us that we were many thousands of feet above the level of the sea.

Notwithstanding the discomforts of living on the "Roof of the World," Tibet is a land of astounding beauty, and of immense interest to the traveller. The cynic perhaps will say that it has the advantage of being cut off from civilisation, for it is surrounded by mountains the highest in the world, which effectually shut it off from India on the south, China and Mongolia on the east and north-east, Eastern Turkistan on the north, and Kashmir and Nepal on the west. In addition to possessing the highest mountain in the world, many of the greatest rivers on the earth's surface have their source of origin in the Hermit Kingdom. The Tsang-po runs almost laterally from west to east across the country, emerging in Assam in the Brahmaputra.

Tibet is the only country that possesses a theocratic

form of Government, the only country that is ruled over by a god, who is incarnate in the person of the head of the Yellow School of Lamaism. Tibet possesses few roads, the western and northern portions of the country are barren and sparsely populated, feudalism is rampant everywhere in spite of the undoubted democratic spirit of the people as a whole, the matriarchal state obtains in many parts of the land, the mean or average elevation is 15,000 feet above the level of the sea, while there is no more religious people extant than the Tibetans. The country, indeed, is probably the most unique in the whole world.

One can wander over the so-called plains of Tibet and scarcely maintain the same altitude for five minutes at a time. One can walk for miles without coming in contact with water, a habitation, a human being, or an animal. The dignity and quietude of the deserted valleys, the majesty of the mountains, the virgin snow lying in scattered patches on the ground and the summits of untrodden mountains that encompass one on all sides, the cruel winds that penetrate the thickest clothes and make life almost intolerable, the resplendent stars that sparkle like diamonds and awaken in one feelings of wonder and admiration—all these things have conspired to make of the Tibetans one of the most remarkable and interesting people in the world.

One emerges from the heated plains of India with their marvellous flora and fauna to the desolation and loneliness of a land where a coarse barley grows in conjunction with a few hardy vegetables, where the yak supplies not only the fuel for cooking its own flesh, but of heating the hovels of the peasants and the homes of the better classes. The dwellings of the peasants consist of dried loam taken from the plains of the country around.

During the day, the sun beats down fierce rays, but not on grass, or meadows, or lanes, or woodland tracks, or trees, or sweet dells. There are no rose gardens, no cherry orchards, no palm trees, no orange blossoms in the northern, western, or southern parts of the Forbidden Land of Tibet, generally speaking.

For mystical training, the study of the eternal question of the Hereafter, symbols and parables, spiritualist séances, astrological beliefs, prophecies, etc., there is no country in the world where religious ideals have a more potent influence than Tibet. It is the things of eternity that count most in the Hermit Kingdom, in spite of the spiritual atrophy of the people. One does not look to men and women of fine intelligence to prove to us the nature of the Hereafter, if we did, it is doubtful that the spiritual emotions would ever be satisfied. The fact that many of the Lamas of Tibet are very ignorant men enable them to exert that necessary influence that satisfies the conditions of the people. To us the great tragedy of Tibet is its isolation from the rest of the world. This isolation has bred in the people and their rulers a conservatism that is almost incapable of uprooting. All the evils of a mediæval priestcraft are everywhere obvious in Tibet.

CHORTENS, PRAYER FLAGS AND DEVIL DANCES.

One of the first things that strikes a visitor to Lamaist countries is the *Chorten*, literally "receptacle for offerings," found everywhere, and not confined solely to monasteries and their precincts. It may be made of metal, stone, clay, or wood. Originally, Chortens were prepared for the reception of sacred relics or the remains of Lamas, but to-day they may be constructed in memory of some well-known Lama who lies buried in a distant part of the country, or to commemorate a notable achievement or event in the neighbourhood of a monastery, or in the monastery itself. Exoterically, the Chorten symbolises the five elements into which man's physical body is resolved after his passing. The solid plinth typifies the solidity of the earth, and thus the element earth. Upon it is set a hemisphere representing the water drop, or the element water. Topping this is a cylindrical, or spire-like flame, representing fire. This is capped by a crescent, like the inverted bowl of the sky, symbolical of the element air. Above is a lead-shaped object tapering in flame into space, the element ether. Esoterically, the Chorten symbolises "the way of Enlightenment," the four planes of being, the physical, astral, mental, and spiritual. Thus from the earth (its base) upwards through the Thirteen Bodhisat Heavens to "the beyond Nature," or Nirvana, where it becomes lost in the Voidness.

The Prayer, or more properly the Praising Wheels, vary in size from the small ones carried in the hands of the devout, to those of larger dimensions found in every monastery in Tibet. Esoterically, they symoblise "the Turning of the Wheel of the Good Law," that is, the sacred teachings of the Lord Buddha. They are believed by the pious to produce an atmosphere of such psychic power that every evil influence is vanquished in their turning. Inside every such instrument is to be found a number of rolls of paper tightly packed together, on which are inscribed the prayer of the Dalai Lama, and each turn of the wheel repeats the sentence as many times as it is inscribed. One Prayer Wheel may contain as many as a thousand inscriptions of "Om! ma-ni padme Hum!" and as it is considered the duty of every Tibetan to twirl the wheel regularly every day, the amount of "merit" thus achieved is enormous.

Prayer Flags are also a feature of the country. They may be seen flying high above the walls of the monasteries, in courtyards, on the roofs of Tibetan buildings, and even in the fields during harvest time. On each is inscribed a petition, and the wind that flutters the pieces of paper or linen on which the petition is written, carries the prayer to the ears of the gods. When the prayers have become obliterated by the action of the wind, rain, etc., they are said to have been answered, and new ones are attached to the tops of the poles or sticks, the occasion being made a solemn and religious function.

In the centre of a road, the visitor to Tibet will occasionally stumble across a prayer wall, on which is drawn pictures of the Buddha to come, saints, and other figures of the Lamaist religion. Chipped into some of these walls of stone and clay is the customary prayer of Tibet. It is necessary, when passing any of these structures, to keep them on the right-hand side. When going round any religious building in Tibet, one should always move "clock wise," that is, from left to right. This is also the orthodox way of twirling a Prayer Wheel.

The so-called "Devil Dance" is an institution of some antiquity in Tibet. Naturally it has undergone a number of modifications since the introduction of Buddhism into the country.

As a spectacle, the Devil Dances of Tibet are most picturesque. In the main, they represent either some historical, legendary, or mythological event associated with the past and present religions of the country, and their variants, in which the "good" spirits vanquish the "evil" ones. But we did not always agree with the Tibetan standards of "goodness" and "badness," any more than we agree with the Western varieties as exemplified by the seven deadly virtues, etc. It occasionally appeared to us that the "bad" Tibetan spirits were more courageous and determined in all they did than the "good" ones, who every now and then prayed to the gods for aid and protection instead of relying on their own efforts to overcome their difficulties. There were few seif-respecting characters portrayed in the play that we were privileged to witness, and which, incidentally, was given in our honour at the Samada Monastery. We were invited to occupy a raised dais, or throne, which common courtesy forbade us refuse. It was the first occasion we had such an honour conferred upon us, and we sincerely hope, the last. We did not feel at all comfortable receiving homage from the local dignitaries, who bowed and scraped and kissed our dirty boots. The re-incarnated Lama of the Monastery was very kind to us, however, and invited criticisms of the performance.

From one o'clock in the afternoon until dewy eve we were entertained by a varied number of masked men and boys, clothed in appallingly wonderful costumes. The figures danced to slow and not unpleasing music. The dancers seemed to remain perfectly erect the while they were moving forward. There was little movement of the body as a whole, no haste, just a slow and dignified step without any apparent bending of the knees. The masks were of enormous size, and out of all proportion to the bodies of the performers. Among them we recognised Ku, the king of ogres, bloody of mien; Tag, the ferocious, man-eating tiger; Teu, the mischievous thief monkey; Seng-gye, the lion whose skin was white; Lang, the red-bull, and finally the Yak, indigenous to Tibet, with gigantic horns. After the appearance of these animals, there entered the graveyard ghouls, all wearing masks of human skulls. These were quickly followed by the Sa-chak-pa, or demons of the earth, and the A-tsa-ra, or buffoons. The majority of these two latter carried in their hands a number of human bones, which they very kindly rattled for our pleasure as they passed before us in solemn procession. All the evil spirits were armed with swords, bows, and arrows, and the colouring effects changed according to the needs of the moment. When joy and gladness were to be typified, the colours were many and variegated, indeed, resplendent, but when sadness and sorrow came the way of the performers, all was changed to dull drab colours.

The dance we witnessed was that of the "Black Hats." The story centred round the killing of a very bad king of Tibet, one Lang-ma Dar-ma, who wanted to banish Buddhism from the sacred land of Tibet. Pal-dor-jé, a Lama attached to the Monastery at Lha-lung, had been chosen from among a number of other saintly personages, to murder the king in order that Buddhism should remain the national faith of Tibet. So one day he disguised himself as a strolling minstrel, and he sang so well outside the castle of the king that the monarch invited the Lama into the royal palace. In his ample sleeves, the Lama had hidden some bows and arrows. As soon as he found himself in the royal presence, he shot the king dead, and succeeded in escaping. The murderer—we are assuming, of course, that he was such—was later canonised, and is now a saint in the Lamaist calendar.

The performance, let it be recorded, was not a tragedy as some readers may surmise. On the contrary, it was a pantomime, or a comedy. It evoked roars of laughter from the very large audience present, an audience that had to stand, that occupied the courtyard of the monastery, and even parts of the roof thereof, to say nothing of the walls.

After the "show," we congratulated each of the performers in person, shaking hands with all of them. To show their appreciation of our courtesy, they extended their tongues wide out of their mouths. There were about forty performers, and we presented the re-incarnated Lama—a god in his own particular sphere —with a sum equivalent to about twenty shillings, with which he appeared delighted. Samada Monastery is one of the poorest in Tibet.

PHARI, THE FOUL.

We had not been ten minutes in Phari when we were visited by the Jong-pön, or Governor of the district. He was accompanied by a retinue of servants, his visit to us being a State one. We found him to be a young man, tall, sleek in appearance, and suffering from anæmia. It being strictly forbidden to smoke in Tibet, the first of a rather formidable series of requests from our honoured guest was for a box of our best cigarettes, always provided that His Holiness the Dalai Lama was never made acquainted with our "generosity." One box did not satisfy the Jong-pön—he grabbed five in all, and looked for more. As each box contained some two hundred and fifty pieces, he did not fare very badly in this respect. Everything he saw, the Jong-pön wanted. He was one of the greediest men it has been our great misfortune to meet. From the first we took a violent dislike to him. However, we presented him with various other things, including a silk jumper for one of his wives, a pair of silk stockings for another, a hatchet, nails, biscuits, tea, sugar, coffee, a gramophone and records, a Zeiss opera glass, a medicine chest containing pills and powder, a Kodak camera, plates, and developing material. If we had presented him with the world, however, he would have wanted the moon also. He took his gifts as a matter of course. He felt himself entitled to everything he could get. During the various presentations, we talked of the virtues of our mothers and fathers, grandmothers and grandfathers, uncles and aunts, nephews and nieces. We were assured that Tibet had been looking forward to our visit, our name and fame were household words in the Forbidden Land. We were free to go where we pleased, and when we informed the Jong-pön that our movemeants were restricted by order of the Government of India, his reply was that the Indian Government had no business to place any restrictions on our movements! We exchanged scarves. These scarves are about a yard long, and are called *Khatags*. No Tibetan would dream of meeting a man in a higher social position or paying a visit without one of these scarves in his possession, which he presents immediately on coming in contact with him. Another very polite method of giving expression to one's feelings for a superior person is to thrust the tongue wide out of the mouth. A European member of our staff, not understanding this peculiar custom, roundly boxed the ears of one of his carriers when the latter desired to show his profound respect for the White Man. Offended dignity had to be toned down, and it took us nearly an hour to soothe wounded pride.

We accepted the invitation of the Jong-pön to dine

at the Phari Fort. We had to climb some very rickety steps that lacked banisters, to reach the abode of our host. It was so dark, and the stairs were so treacherous, that we were nearly precipitated into the yak shed below, some one hundred and fifty feet under the State apartments of the Jong-pön. When we at last reached the quarters of our host, we were introduced to some of his wives. The boy who served the soup was suffering from a rather severe attack of nose running. Fortunately the room was very dark, and we managed to make use of a lovely large hole in the floor, down which went soup, tea, biscuits and everything else that was handed to us by him. The yaks below no doubt derived some benefit therefrom. We all had to sit crossed-legged, and after two hours of it, we asked permission to stretch ourselves. The repast took over four hours to consume, at the end of which time we were all suffering tortures. Our heads were splitting, we longed for the crisp, fresh air. But before that could be got, we had to be introduced to the deputy Jong-pön. So we were escorted to another department, where we chatted for an hour or so. Midnight came, we made our usual apologies and excuses, and with profuse thanks, retired.

The accumulated filth of ages has raised the level of the thoroughfare of Phari so high that the roofs of the houses are now almost on a level with the streets. The consequence is that the Pharians have to enter their dwellings by a passage cut through the layer of garbage to their doors.

When a lady of the town threw the contents of a receptacle over the person of one of our servants, accidentally, it is true (the Tibetans are one of the politest peoples on the face of the Earth) his anger may be imagined, and things began to look ugly for him when the whole town collected to join issue in the squabble. The matter, however, was amicably settled by an exchange of apologies, and the presentation of a powder-puff by us to the lady who had caused the trouble. We pointed out to her, however, when making the presentation, that to be efficacious, the face should first be washed. Here we put our foot into it, and the row we had just quelled, broke out afresh. We were told that we could keep our powder and puff, that we were no gentlemen, that we had insulted the good lady, etc. Pray, when had a woman of Phari been so indiscreet as to permit a drop of water to dirty her face! Did we want the good woman to be the subject of gossip and scandal? Were we not aware that when one loses one's dirt in Tibet, self-respect and virtue go with it? Hastily glancing at the powder box, we pretended that the preparation it contained was different to the usual brand, that we had erred in believing it was necessary for the dirt to be removed before application. So the lady eventually accepted the powder and puff, and proceeded to apply it without another word of remonstrance. In a moment or two, she had used up the contents, and like Oliver Twist, wanted more. On the morrow of this little incident, about thirty women presented themselves at the Dak Bungalow in quest of powder and puffs, of which we had brought some dozens with us from home for distribution. Before we left Phari, it had become the fashion of some of the women there to powder and puff the dirt that covered their faces, and we were honoured with the name of, "The White Man from across the Silvery Waters and the Snow-clad Mountains who makes brown women yellow."

Travel to-day in Tibet is crude, to say the least. There is little or no comfort for the jaded traveller, and save for the Dak Bungalows erected by the Indian Government for the convenience of the Sahibs, and a few outhouses for their servants, there is no accommodation. Not that many Europeans travel in Tibet. Indeed, since the land first became known to Western civilisation, it is doubtful that more than one hundred White Men have been privileged to visit the country. Fleas and bugs abound. This need not occasion surprise, since the people, generally speaking, are not given to washing themselves. The clothes the Tibetan peasants wear have literally grown on them since they were infants in their mothers' arms, the custom being to add a piece of cloth to the original rags donned by them in their infancy, up to the time they have attained full stature, when the process naturally ceases. The stench of the so-called towns is due in part to the dirt of the inhabitants and the absence of latrines and the more primitive form of drainage. The food of the people consists principally of raw meat and a coarse barley. The contemptuous dislike of foreigners everywhere has no doubt been accentuated by the events of 1904, when the Younghusband Military Expedition invaded the country, and dictated terms of peace at Lhasa. There are no roads worthy of the name. Where these have been erected, the telegraph lines indicate the traveller's route.

The emptiness of the land around is appalling. For miles on end scarcely a human habitation is met with. Since we left Darjeeling, we have detected traces of oil, iron, and copper. But the country is barren. A poor soil has decimated whole populations. A silence broods over the countryside which is without water, trees, or vegetation save that of a stunted barley.

In the villages the peasants are indescribably poor. Disease is rampant. The poor Tibetans live in the utmost squalor and misery, little better than the yaks they breed. In a country raised so high above the level of the sea, which gives a cold climate and so few of Nature's bounties, their lives are probably the hardest in the world. Yet to all appearances they are wonderfully well. We were told that starvation is unknown among them. The women are invariably plump and stumpy. They are a very industrious people. Up with the sun, they retire with its setting. They light no lamps by night, they sleep and eat in apartments that in most cases are below the ground level. Even visitors sleep in the same room as their hosts and hostesses. Comfort is unknown to them, they know that their lot will never be more than what it is. To eat, to drink, to sleep, to work, to have children—beyond these the peasants of Tibet have no ambitions. The vast majority of them never leave the village they are born in.

Tibet is supposedly a Buddhist country, where the taking of life, even for food, is to all good Buddhists a sin. We saw a yak killed. A "religious" ceremony was performed on behalf of the beast before it was sent to its doom, and on enquiring the reason, we were told that the ceremony would ensure the animal's re-birth in a higher state of existence: Thus the loss of its life was a gain to the yak.

Once a mighty Empire, Tibet to-day is a comparatively small country if we exclude the Chang-t'ang, or "No Man's Land" that lies to the north, and Chinese Tibet in the east. Tibet proper is not more than 200,000 square miles in area, much of which is uninhabited and uninhabitable, sparsely populated with probably not more than five million souls all told, who either live in out-of-the-way monasteries or congregate in the towns, of which Lhasa, Shigatse, Gyantse, and Phari are the principal.

The Bhutanese yogin who invited us to accompany him to the summit of the "mysterious" mountain of Chu-mi was to all appearances everything that a yogin should be. We first met him dressed in the conventional garb of a yogin, a piece of cotton about the loins, in one of the fastnesses that separate Tibet from Bhutan, on the main Bhutan-Phari trade route. He looked a man of about sixty years of age; he had sparkling eyes and wore a beard that covered his otherwise naked chest. Through our interpreter, we learned that the yogin had lived in the hollow of a mountain for over twenty years, some 15,500 feet above sea-level, that he was endowed with great faith, and his heart was overflowing with sympathy and love for his fellow creatures. From his bleak home, he could look down upon the world, and commiserate with long-suffering humanity, for whom he had feelings of the deepest pity. He had enjoyed the advantage of being taught by holy men, he had tasted of the bitterness of life, but now, in the delightful solitude of his mountain retreat, he was slowly obtaining emancipation from the Wheel of Life. He did not think he had yet attained to full growth, spiritually speaking, and believed he was destined to suffer many more re-births before he attained Nirvana. He had been favoured by gods and spirits, and was able to manifest supernormal powers at will. Life had long since lost its terrors for him, he was in a state of blissful communion with many of the gods of the Tibetan Pantheon. He had but one remaining desire, and that was attaining to full spiritual knowledge and experience. Of the few wild beasts that came his way, none had done violence to his person. On the contrary, he was able to render good service to these creatures by preaching unto them the Law. Some had been known to sit at his feet and purr their grateful thanks for the knowledge he imparted to them. He had acquired power over both men and beasts, and such was his command of the elements that he could turn the lightning from its path, and make nought of the roar of the thunder. He could sleep in a standing attitude on one lèg without support of any kind. He could float in the air and walk on the water, and at his will, flames of fire and jets of water would emanate from his body. Of food and drink and clothes, he had long since discarded the practice of eating and drinking and wearing any apparel.

The peak of Chu-mi rises some 16,450 feet above sea-level, or 1,850 feet above the plain of Phari. It had never previously been visited by a white man. The yogin was anxious for us to make the ascent, as it would give prestige to the eminence!

The morning we made the ascent was bitterly cold. The yogin was the first to attain the summit. Obviously he was familiar with the road. While the European was standing gazing at the stupendous precipices before him, precipices that cannot fail to inspire awe and wonder, to say nothing of emotion in the onlooker, the yogin was talking about the stern realities of the mighty Himalaya—depths and heights, barren rocks, cold, snow, winds, treeless deserts, and far, far below, many a surging cataract. We had heard of the many things the yogin could do—would he float in the air and disappear from mortal vision for the benefit of the White Man? We were asked to watch him for a moment or two. With a few peculiar movements of the body, the yogin disappeared in a very mysterious manner. We could not vouch for any feat in levitation, but he certainly did disappear on a piece of level ground with no obstacles within fifty feet of the observer. No trace of the yogin could be found. Then, suddenly, out of the ground as it were, he re-appeared. We asked him how it was done, and received the reply that we should have to re-incarnate ten thousand times ten thousand before we could make such an approach to excellence in things spiritual!

OVER THE TREMO LA INTO BHUTAN.

There are no indications to hand in Phari to lead the traveller to imagine that much beauty lies beyond the Tremo La. Yet a few hours' ride will bring him into a land of rapidly-moving waters, huge forests, a wild race of people, scattered monasteries, and a soil capable of yielding the treasures of the earth. In addition to being the filthiest place in the whole world, Phari is one of the most desolate spots in Tibet, practically a desert, where a stunted barley forces its unwilling way through the surface of the plains over which a number of yaks and wild foxes and wolves sport themselves daily. Situated some 14,300 feet above the level of the sea, Phari is best known to travellers for the view one obtains of one of the most sacred mountains in the Hermit Kingdom—that of Mount Chumolhari, the dear Lady of the Snows.

The Tremo La lies in the mediæval, old-world State of Bhutan, famous for the number and violence of its thunderstorms. As we were not officially allowed to deviate from the path plotted out for us by the Indian Government, and Bhutan lay outside our route, to salve our conscience we asked for and obtained permission of the Jong-pön of Phari to make the excursion. Little odd jobs of this kind His Excellency was always prepared to do for a consideration.

It goes without saying that we had to heavily grease the palm of the Jong-pön for the various permissions we obtained from him to go where our fancy listed, the majority of which he had no business to give, and which it was tacitly agreed between us should be immediately repudiated by each side in the event of discovery by either the Tibetan or the Indian Governments. Once he hinted that we could sneak off to Mount Everest if we so desired, but the fee he demanded for this stunt was so heavy that we decided to make no attempts to scale its heights, which he assured us would add lustre to our name and bring renown to Tibet. Being clairvoyant, he said he could *see* we would not make such a fearful mess of the job as did those who but a few months before, tried to attain the summit of Everest.* The gods of Everest were revengeful gods, yet they were very favourably disposed towards our person. But we were not parting with a thousand rupees, although we were game enough for almost anything else.†

To resume our journey to Bhutan. It was early morning, and the orb of day had not yet cast its rays over the dung-heap of Phari when we set out for the Tremo La, some 16,500 feet above sea-level. We had supplied ourselves and our pony with sufficient provisions and fodder for three days' stay in the adjoining country of Bhutan. The route was absolutely unknown to us, and we left everything to the god of Chance.

Looking back on the plains beneath, the village of Phari, with its high and frowning fort, appeared

* He was referring to the 1922 Mount Everest Expedition.

† While travelling in the Baltic States in 1926, Mr. G. E. O. Knight, who had at that time successfully penetrated Bolshevik Russia in disguise, received an urgent offer to proceed to India and make an attempt on Mount Everest (also in disguise) for the purpose of ascertaining the fate of Mallory and Irvine. But his over-zealous fellow Fellow of the Royal Geographical Society let the cat out of the bag, and the project was abruptly abandoned.

enveloped in a cloud of yellow vapour in the breaking dawn. The peasants had not yet turned out to work. The smoke around was due to the combustion of yak dung, this being the only fuel with which the poor Tibetans cook their coarse food and heat their wretched hovels. The Pharians are living under strict feudal conditions, in spite of which they seem a happy and contented lot. They are dreadfully dirty, the dirt in some cases rolling off their faces in appreciable lumps. Phari itself is built upon the refuse of its inhabitants of centuries old gathering.

As we could find no track to our destination, we watched and waited for someone who might be passing that way. As no soul came in sight, we decided to leave everything to our pony's discretion, and we were justified in so doing. Three hours after leaving Phari we reached the summit of the Tremo La from which a magnificent view of the Himalaya was obtained. The sun was now well above the horizon. Almost facing us was a wonderful mountain, Mount Chotokre called by the Bhutanese. The descent into Bhutan on the far off side of the Tremo La entered a gorge more stupendous than that of the Red Gorge in Tibet, which is dry all the year round, whereas that of which we are now writing contains the waters of the river Pa, emptying themselves into a number of deep valleys that lie scattered in every direction.

Here we had a curious and interesting experience. We noted that our pony had suddenly become very restive. In fact, we had some difficulty in restraining it from bolting. Looking about for the cause, we saw a pack of wolves in front of us. Both rider and pony stood motionless. So did the wolves who barred our further progress. We coaxed our pony who by now was gazing rather curiously at the creatures. We had christened our pony Nellie, and we used to hold conversations together. On this particular occasion, we said, "Say, Nellie, you know that we seldom carry arms or ammunition about our person. We consider ourselves good sportsmen, too. Are you game enough to charge down this precipitous mountain and scatter the wolves, or would you rather await events?" Nellie neighed, and this we took to mean a negative in so far as scattering the wolves was concerned. Nellie kept on neighing; she almost burst into opera, in fact. Presently we were constrained to join in the song, and gave a really magnificent selection from Verdi's *Rigoletto*—something about women being false, and fickle, and changeable. The effect on the wolves was magical. Whether it was our horrible rendering of the beautiful Italian language, or the fine neighing of Nellie, or the combined efforts of rider and pony, will certainly never be known. The wolves, however, scattered before we had time to finish the chorus, the climax to a really fine setting.

Which reminds us of a concert we were asked to give at the bidding of the Jong-pön of Phari. It was really more of a sing-song than a concert. A bottle of whisky and cigarettes were the instruments employed. His Excellency had intimated the pleasure it would give him and his concubines if we would run over to his official residence and sing to him. We enquired through our interpreter if he would prefer classical or common music. In reply he asked for the whisky we had brought with us. He drank this neat, smoked cigarette after cigarette, and when he was about two-thirds fuddled and the room was smoked out, we were called upon to oblige. We began with a selection from Gounod's *Faust*—something about a tender moon and stars in heaven. After that we enquired what impression our efforts had made upon His Excellency. He complained of a pain in the head! Would we oblige with something more appealing to the emotions? We chose *Tipperary*, and made him learn the chorus. He was singing it long after midnight when we were tucked between the blankets in the Dak Bungalow of Phari.

When we saw our way was no longer disputed by the wolves, Nellie took us very cautiously down the Tremo La, the paths of which consisted of a series of twistings and turnings even more bewildering than those that took us up the Nathu La when we bid farewell to the Roof of the World. Before us were many beautiful waterfalls and cataracts. We soon found ourselves passing through some lovely forests, and with Nellie as the Leader of the Expedition, she naturally wanted to taste of luxuries not to be found on the plains of her native Tibet. So she had a good feed while we squatted on the ground looking at some dragon flies and other insects. After a while we re-mounted, and went casually on, caring little where we went until it dawned upon us we were approaching a village. High up in the distance we noted a huge monastery. Now we thought it time to draw rein and retrace our steps. Nellie had no desire to return to Phari, however, and purposely lost her way several times. However, we insisted, and after a leisurely going, we arrived once more at the Tremo La where we rested for the night. Early next morning we got back safely to Phari, and no one was the wiser for the escapade.

A MEETING WITH A DISTINGUISHED EXPLORER.

Brig.-General Sir G. Pereira arrived in Phari looking very ill. It was impossible for him to mount the few steps leading to the dining-room, so we helped him up. He was very lame. However, we soon had him comfortably installed before the fire, and he revived considerably.

Sir George told us that he left Pekin in January, 1921, and travelled southwards to Tai-yen-fu, thence by cart to Shansi, thence to Hoyang via the Hoang-ho or Yellow River, where he had a long conversation with General Wu Pei Fu, whom he regarded as China's greatest man. He paid a visit to Sianfu, the old capital of China, climbed one of the five sacred mountains of China, by name Hwashan, and proceeded next to Tatsien-fu, suffering much from frostbite in the meanwhile. Up the Min River he entered the province of Kansu, where he met an old friend in the person of the Prince of Choui, who offered him hospitality and protection. Next Sir George passed through Sining-fu, a Mohammedan province, and thence on to Dangar, where he made final preparations for his long and perilous journey through Tibet via Lhasa, the capital. At Jekundo he met Madame Nëel, a French Buddhist lady travelling in Tibet, the only European in his journey of six thousand miles from Pekin. Besides being the first European to enter Lhasa from China since Huc in 1845, of the six thousand four hundred miles from Pekin to the capital of Tibet, he told us he had actually accomplished three thousand eight hundred of them on foot—not a bad feat for a man 58 years of age.

During our conversation, Sir George broke off more than once with references to the Derby! Were we interested in horses? Had we ever seen the Derby? If not, why not? He would return to England and see the Derby of 1924, at whatever cost to him. Then he must cross the continent of South America and perhaps Africa from West to East. We told him quite frankly we were not interested in racing, that we had never seen a horse-race in our life, and in all probability never would see one. We are afraid that Sir George thought us a fool. Then he explained he was suffering from gastric ulcers. His throat also was "a bit queer." We offered him the best room in the Bungalow. He would not accept it; he preferred to sleep in the servants' quarters, and in the servants' quarters he did sleep. We offered him blankets and bedding, but he had his own, "although they were a bit dirty." We half carried him down the steps at eleven o'clock at night.

There are few white men now living who can claim to have visited the City of the Gods. Among them may be mentioned that distinguished scholar, Sir Charles Bell, the greatest living authority on Tibet; Sir Francis Younghusband, also a distinguished scholar and authority on the East; Col. F. M. Bailey, Dr. W. M. McGovern, and a handful of others. Dr. McGovern had a very bad reception in Lhasa because he went as an uninvited guest, sneaking in by the back door, as it were. But he showed commendable enterprise and determination in all that he did. Naturally his adventure was little understood or appreciated by those who regard Tibet as their special preserve. The expedition of which we were the Leader made futile attempts to visit Lhasa by legitimate means. Brig.-General Sir G. Pereira experienced no difficulty whatever in getting to Lhasa since he had both the moral and material support of the Indian Government. Naturally we were a bit sore that a titled Englishman should be allowed, without let or hindrance, to enter Lhasa while we innocents were ordered to quit the country. The General, on his return to India, was in a position to furnish valuable information to the British Government regarding the military, economic, and political conditions of China, etc.

Pereira was not very favourably impressed by Lhasa, and he could not understand those people who have weaved a web of romance, quite unwarranted, round the capital. As a matter of fact, there is little doubt that he was happy to turn his back upon the city. He was not to be envied, he told us, for having visited Lhasa, one of the least interesting places he had seen. What struck the General about the place was its filth! After two or three days, he said, it began to pall, he felt confined, he loved the free and open-air life of the country, he could not understand why men live in monasteries, twirling prayer wheels and counting their beads. The General was a Roman Catholic. He was fond of shooting.

The Potola did not greatly impress the General. It looked much bigger than it really is because of its being built upon a hill. The General assured us there were many residences in the West End of London much more imposing than is the residence of the Dalai Lama. His first impression of the building was that of a huge fortress.

What gave the capital of Tibet its romance? Possibly its inaccessibility, coupled with the fact that the traveller has to traverse the most glorious mountains in the world to reach it.

But Romance, no, it is not to be found in Lhasa! So thought Pereira.

MONASTERIES.

We have said that Tibet is a land of Monasteries. The history of the country comprises in the main a series of records of the founding of Monasteries and Temples, and their endowments by the State, etc.

There are over twenty different dissenting Buddhist sects in the land, and the majority of these comprise those that are attached to the Yellow Caps, or Progressive School of Lamaism, and the minority that are adherents of the Red Caps, or Retrogressive School. The former has become the dominant party since the middle of the seventeenth century, and His Holiness the Dalai Lama, the Conqueror or Victor of Life, is the Spiritual Head of this Church.

According to official statistics, there are now about 1,110 Monasteries distributed throughout the country that belong to the Yellow School, with a total population of over half a million monks, and some 1,400 Monasteries belonging to the Red School, with a total population of a quarter of a million of monks. Speaking approximately, there are some 2,500 Monasteries in Tibet all told, with three-quarters of a million monks belonging to all schools of thought in the Tibetan Pantheon.

Every third boy in a family is sent to a Monastery.

The Yellow Cap Church Lamas take the vow of celibacy, and this circumstance prevents them coming in contact with women.

There are but few Convents in Tibet, and the number of nuns therefore is small. The total number of

Convents throughout the country is approximately twenty-five, and the number of nuns living in them not more than 500.

The Monastery at Samada was founded in the year 1675. Samada is a small village, on the road to Gyantse, and contains about 200 villagers, all of whom are wretchedly poor. There are over 300 monks in this Monastery, which is built round the commonplace courtyard. Generally speaking, the exterior has a very dilapidated appearance. We were escorted over the place, and shown a golden image of Maitreya, the Loving One, the coming Buddha. The figure is internally of clay, and externally gilded. We were all enjoined to perform a circuit around this image in order to derive "merit." The effigy was seated, and legs were down. We were told the image was supposed to be teaching the Law. In close proximity were life-size statues of Kushi Khan and Milarepa. Several mythological warriors in divers attitudes next claimed our attention. In the chapel was a figure of the Buddha, images of the Buddhas and Bodhisattvas gilded over, besides numerous tapestries, pictures, and images of different Temples. A fine picture of the Buddha vanquishing Mara, the Evil One, and a host of demons, several life-like images, the goddess Kali on horseback, her legs being tied by a chain, were next pointed out to our party. We were ushered into the library of sacred books where we found collections of the Kangyur and the Tangyur, or Buddhist canons.

The Monastery is named in Tibetan *Göm-pa*, meaning a solitary place or hermitage. Most of the Monasteries in Tibet are situated in solitary places, or at some distance from the villages, the idea being that their inmates shall escape the temptations of the multitude. There are Monasteries in the Swiss Alps that have been placed there for the same reasons. It must not be supposed that the situation of the various Monasteries in Tibet or elsewhere has reference to penance—what the monks desire is meditation, and this can best be secured through isolation.

The vast majority of the Monasteries in Tibet are

over 14,000 feet above the level of the sea, and there are thousands of monks living in them who have never seen a White Man, who know nothing of an outside world, who cannot read nor write, whose horizon extends no further than the grounds of the Monastery. The site chosen is usually both commanding and picturesque, and some have been so built that they overhang a dangerous precipice. Many of these buildings are so remote that they are inaccessible to ordinary travellers in the country. The cave hermitages are generally natural caverns, tenanted by wandering ascetics who have either lived in Monasteries and found the life too dull, or are men on the tramp to some sacred spot in the Forbidden Land. The names of Monasteries in general are either place names or of a religious significance. Some are derived from words that mean "The Place of Perfect Peace," "The Support of the Lord Buddha's Precepts," "The Monastery of Most Excellent Bliss," "The Monastery of the Lofty Summit," etc.

Every site chosen for a Monastery is consecrated before a stone is laid. There is the ceremony of the laying of the foundation stone at which prayers are offered to the tutelary deity.

The Monastery at Sera, near Lhasa, contains more than 10,000 monks. Many of the Monasteries are larger than the villages in which they have been established. The majority of the Monasteries are built of stone taken out of the mountain side.

The great Temple and Monastery called Ba Kor Chode—the Golden Temple—is the principal object of interest in Gyantse. Gyantse is one of the four principal cities of Tibet, and most of its inhabitants are living in the Monastery, which consists of tiers of buildings terracing the hillside of the city, the whole being surrounded by a battlemented wall nearly a mile in circumference.

In the porch of the Monastery are to be seen colossal statues of the four great Kings, the Guardians of the Four Quarters, painted respectively green, red, yellow, and white, each of whom has ninety-one sons who share in the privileges enjoyed by their parents. Each helps to guard the ten regions of space. Each King has eight omnipotent Generals, who have power over the lesser gods of the mountains, forests, etc. There are also some allegorical paintings on the walls of the porch, among them a Wheel of Life, disciples, and saints, and fearsome looking demons. The most interesting object in the Temple itself is a fantastic image measuring fifteen feet in height, and which, Buddha-like, sits cross-legged. It is that of Maitreya. Rows of cushions were arranged on the floor for the use of the priests on ceremonial occasions. Every visitor was required to take off his boots before entering the Temple, as is customary in Buddhist countries generally, and we had to move round the building in the proper manner from left to right, or clockwise.

Next we were introduced to a rather forbidding-looking place, devoted to the arts of black magic. In this dungeon, for such it proved to be, reside all the gods, demons, etc., of the Bön, or indigenous religion of the country. Among the most conspicuous objects were an image with a number of arms, the goddess Kali, a female demon riding what appeared to be a horse, whose saddle girths were made of human skulls. Stuffed birds rotting with age, human skins, weapons, skulls, braziers, and a host of uncanny-looking implements and instruments, constituted the exhibits of this strange Museum. The guide informed us that the place was used for the practice of black magic, including the finding of the philosopher's stone!

The Tibetans claim to possess the power of prophecy. They certainly did predict with commendable good luck the year of the termination of the Great War. So did many English seers, politicians among them. Many years before the event happened, the Tibetans prophesied their country would be overrun by a barbarian horde. The Younghusband Military Expedition of 1904 is now a matter of history. But was it not Bacon who said, "Men mark what they hit, but mark not what they miss"? We shall not say on how many occasions we caught the Tibetans tripping. There was an old Tibetan Lama who prophesied our demise within six months of our departure from his country! That is some time ago now—much more than six months. In a country where men are making hundreds of prophecies daily, would it not be rather surprising if some of them failed to materialise?

Every visitor to Tibet has noted the coincidences between Lamaism and that of the Oriental and Latin Churches. Let us say there is no question of a common dogma. The resemblances deal only with ritualistic details, such as the cross, the mitre, choir singing, benedictions, celibacy, spiritual retreats, etc. Monasticism indeed is developed to a far greater extent in Tibet than in any country in the world.

Voluntary entombment is practised rather extensively in Tibet. The entrance to these tombs is built up solidly with stones and mortar, the only opening being a tiny aperture about six inches square, just large enough for the hermit to pass out his hand for his daily food of barley and water. The ascetic remains in total darkness during the whole part of his solitary confinement. He has no means of distinguishing the passing of time, etc., his vows forbid him to see or talk to anyone during his confinement, which may be for seven, fourteen, or twenty-one years, sometimes for life, voluntarily imposed.

SOME CURIOUS TIBETAN BELIEFS.

The ideas prevalent amongst the Tibetans regarding the magic arts, spells and charms, and particularly the belief in the power of certain humans to transform themselves into wild beasts and prey upon their fellow creatures, have been imported into the Hermit Kingdom from India, China, etc., who in turn have received them from other lands. Such superstitions are found everywhere to-day. Each has received its local colouring. In many cases, the original idea has become so distorted that it is difficult to trace its exact home of origin. The human pig of Tibet finds its counterpart in the human tiger of the Malay Peninsula and the human jaguar of South America. There is a story in Tibet that turns upon the Abbess of a very famous Nunnery who claims to have the power of transforming herself and her Nuns into pigs! Some years ago the Eleuths invaded Tibet and laid waste the capital. The Eleuths were Mohammedans. When they came to sack a certain Nunnery the Abbess, in order to save its treasures, transformed herself and her bevy of Nuns into pigs, which grunted so much that it hurt the religious susceptibilities of the raiders, who are said to have retired from the scene in utter disgust. There is the story of the newly-wedded man whose jealousy of his young wife was such that he sought the power of a Lama who conferred upon him the form of a full-grown tiger which waylaid every stranger that left his dwelling. One night the moon was not shining, the wife went out to fetch some water from the river near by, and the human tiger, mistaking his wife for a male visitor, attacked and killed her. When he found he was the cause of his wife's death, the Lama refused to transform him into a human being, and the tiger went forth into the forests of India. One day he was attacked by another tiger, a great, ferocious beast. The human tiger, on account of his superior cunning, got the better of the bargain, and he killed his attacker, only to be killed shortly after by the "ghost" of his late wife.

The European ghost, or "revenant," is not unknown in Tibet. Indeed, the spirits of near ancestors sometime appear in dreams, and express their wishes to the living. But, generally speaking, a ghost is regarded as malicious in Tibet. It often expresses a desire to know what has become of the property it has left behind, and who has taken possession of it. A ghost in Tibet is often more powerful than a living person there, and some of them are actually subject to the same feelings and passions as humans. Other of the Tibetan ghosts may be duped and tricked, but those which cast an evil spell on people may and can be *burned*! For this purpose, eight Lamas are necessary, the ceremony being a most elaborate one, demanding considerable sacrifices on the part of the person who is under the spell of the ghost. The treatment, however, is guaranteed to give the ghost its quietus, and never to curse the victim again.

The cult of man animals, most frequently birds, is probably indigenous to Tibet. These are said to be possessed of certain invisible beings that float in the air. The vulture, therefore, is regarded with considerable reverence in Tibet because it is the bird that feeds upon human corpses, the soul of the departed being borne aloft by these winged creatures. There are certain small animals in Tibet that are invoked to secure good crops, freedom from disease, and other mundane things. There is a class of undefined spirit-helpers who, when called upon, assist the traveller in finding the right direction. The spirit of a dead relative will come to the bereaved in a dream, and will direct the dreamer to some object which needs attention.

The Nagas of the sky, or rain-deities, are propitiated once a year. A great procession is usually formed in all the principal towns in Tibet. High officials pay State visits to the various monasteries, and presents of brick-tea are made to the poor. The various idols are satisfied with offerings of gold, silver and copper. The object of the ceremony, which is one of the most popular in Tibet, is to secure sufficient rain for both crops and animals.

The Adam and Eve of Tibet were a monkey and she-wolf respectively. These married, and the progeny of the pair were miraculously fed by the good spirit of the mountains, or Chenraisi, the Tibetan form of Avalokita, or Brahma of Indian mythology. From their mother's side, the Tibetans have obtained their ferocity, cunning, deceit, etc., and from their father's their love for religion, piety, gentleness, good manners, and other virtues.

A convent we were once privileged to visit was dedicated to Döl-ma, the "Virgin Mother of Mercy," or "She who Hears the Cries of the whole World." This Döl-ma is no other than the Indian goddess of Mercy, Tāra, consort of Avalokita, who is now said to be incarnate in the Dalai Lama. Döl-ma, or Tāra, is the goddess of Mercy and Queen of Heaven of the Chinese. In origin and form, however, she is essentially of Indian origin.

The Nuns were astounded at seeing a white man in their midst, the first they had ever seen. Greatly beloved, they are akin to our Sisters of Mercy. When called, they go forth to succour the sick and dying. We found some of them feeding creatures of the wild, who were quite at home with the Sisters, but who bolted immediately they saw us!

It is always necessary to propitiate the gods of the waters when in the centre of a bridge. It is considered by the Tibetans to be exceedingly discourteous not to throw stones to the water gods. In London, stone-throwing is a legal offence. What gods want with stones is difficult to understand. We were so engrossed when crossing a bridge that we forgot to do our duty and throw the all-necessary stones. We somehow reached the other bank of the river in safety, however. So did all but one of our servants. A Tibetan woman carrier loaded her capacious pockets with chunks of rock, and was obviously taking no risks. She stopped in the centre of the rather shaky bamboo bridge with our beautiful clean bedding and clothing on her back. She was in the act of throwing the last piece of rock when that part of the bridge on which she was standing gave way, and the next we saw of her was in the waters below, floundering about more interested in rescuing her precious load than in her own personal safety. She told us afterward that had we observed the necessary rite she would never have been precipitated in the depths beneath!

There are four modes of burial in Tibet. The most honourable is for the body to be cut up and the pieces distributed to the vultures. Or the corpse may be cast into running water. It may be buried in the earth or cremated. Earth burial is only reserved for people who die from some fell disease, as smallpox; cremation is rarely indulged in save for very high personages and the wealthy who can afford to purchase the necessary fuel. Burial by water necessitates the body being cut up and disembowelled.

The charms, talismans, amulets, and mascots worn by the Tibetans are a feature of the people. Turquoise and amber predominate. Amber beads are worn by some to strengthen their eyes, turquoise is for good luck. Colour, too, has its magical qualities with the people—the red woollen clothes worn by both the men and women is a counter-charm against the Evil Eye. The belief in the Evil Eye is firmly rooted with the Tibetans. It is possessed not only by men and women, but also by animals. Pointing the finger towards the earth is said to be one of the many ways of counteracting the influence of the Evil Eye.

A Lama we met in Yatung had a rosary of human bones about his neck. He told us that it conferred endurance upon him, and, in addition, it was a certain cure for toothache!

As a rule, the Tibetans are exceedingly unclean in their habits. Cooking utensils are seldom washed, while the floors, walls, ceilings, etc., of Tibetan hovels are usually thick with the dirt of generations. There is little or no personal cleanliness about the people. Hundreds of thousands of Tibetans pass through this "vale of tears" without indulging in cutaneous ablution. Living as they do at an average elevation of 15,000 feet above the level of the sea, it is perhaps small wonder that the desire to wash is wanting among them, for this elevation gives a very cold climate. From eleven in the morning until sunset, the infernal winds of Tibet play havoc with the traveller. Even we Europeans, accustomed as we have been to the delights of washing, were pretty hard put to it sometimes when the servants announced that bath was ready, and some of us were known to go without a bath for as long as a month! Of course, we made up for it when we returned to India.

The pillory is as common in Tibet to-day as it was in England in the sixteenth century. Sometimes the law-breaker is both handcuffed and fettered to the pillory, but more often he or she is exposed to public censure with handcuffs or fetters alone. Another form of punishment is to tie the offender to a post, with the neck attached in a frame of wooden boards an inch thick and four feet square. In the centre of the frame is a hole large enough to enclose the neck of the culprit, the boards being then fastened together by ridges and a lock. Flogging invariably follows the condemnation to the pillory, and the number of lashes varies greatly; for some offences as many as eight hundred lashes are administered. No exception to this punishment is made in the case of women, both sexes being equal before the law. Flogging is always done publicly.

Among the peasant population of Tibet there are no very definite ideas possessed by them in regard to the shape and size of the earth, the nature of the stars, winds, rains, clouds, and snow. From all that could be gleaned, there appeared a general agreement that the earth is as flat as the plains of the country, but variations were to be found here and there even in respect to this particular. The notion that Tibet is the earth, and the earth Tibet, is held by the stay-at-homes. Not one of the peasants with whom we held intercourse had any idea of distance, shape or size. The earth "is as large as it looks." A round object was not always round. The idea of length, breadth and thickness was unknown among many of the peasants of Phari and Tuna. A peasant at the former place told us that the earth terminates at the mountain edges, that there are holes in the mountains to permit of the sun, moon, and stars to pass through daily. How like the Greeks of old! The sun, of course, was specially created for the poor Tibetans, who regard it as being made of yak dung. It is replenished daily by the good spirits that watch over the destiny of the Tibetans, and these spirits come every day to earth and take away a sufficiency of yak dung for the following day's consumption. When the last yak has been slaughtered, the sun will " go out."

The moon is sometime a man, sometimes a woman. When half-full, and a shooting star appears in its neighbourhood, it is a man practising archery; when full, it is a she-devil aiding brigands to rob the traveller who chooses night for his journey, in order to escape the machinations of the spirit who brings the biting winds of day to torture him.

The Tibetans are not astronomers, but astrologers. Hundreds of Tibetans believe that the stars are decreasing in numbers, the illusion being due to the terrestrial phenomenon of shooting stars. When all the stars are gone, Tibet will be overrun by a barbarian race.

WE RETURN TO SIKKIM.

Feeling a bit fed up with Darjeeling after our return from Tibet, we decided to leave the hill station one bright January morning for the purpose of paying a visit of respect to some of the gods of Lamaism in Sikkim. Our route lay through a part of Sikkim that was unfamiliar to us. This naturally added zest to our travels. We left without fuss or ostentation with half a dozen Tibetan women carriers and our faithful servant Anqui. We had grown tired of mules and expeditions, and determined on this occasion to do the journey on foot. Our servant did not like the idea of his white master walking twenty miles a day—he said no respectable Sahib had ever undertaken a long and an arduous journey in such circumstances before. It was not the correct thing to do—every Sahib rides in India. Would we reconsider our decision? When we pointed out that we cared nothing, absolutely nothing, for convention, and would go in quest of the gods "on Shanks' pony," Anqui utterly mistook our meaning and had a pony in waiting for us when the hour came for leaving! This we dismissed after attempting to make clear our meaning. Fortunately the boy had a fine sense of humour, and his one topic of conversation *en route* was his failure to understand the connexion between the four legs of Shanks' pony and the two of his revered master. Which reminds us of a letter we received from one of our servants who had fallen ill and was unable to attend to his duties. Translated from Tibetan into English, it ran as follows: "Most High and Revered Sahib, Master of the Sun, Moon and Stars, Brother of the Lord Buddha, Ruler with the seven Kings of the Lands beyond the waters of the Ocean, Greeting. I ask your pardon for sending you this most disgusting letter which confirms my painful illness of a big pain in my belly which my wife says will go away when the next moon comes to pay its respects to Darjeeling. Your most charmed and luscious servant, Dorjé Umdse. I kiss your face, your beautiful white face which ever smiles."

When the next moon did pay its respects to Darjeeling, poor Dorjé Umdse certainly did not see it. He must, we fear, await reincarnation before he again catches a glimpse of our satellite.

We had to strike the valley of the great Rungeet river which divides British Darjeeling from Sikkim, and in so doing, to drop some 6,000 feet. We soon found ourselves in a steamy atmosphere not unlike that which characterises the plains of Bengal, "which dries up our blood and muddles our brains," as one writer has cynically put it. Crossing a fragile bridge which necessitated our throwing some stones into the waters beneath to appease the fury of the demons inhabiting them, and so prevent our destruction, we presently found ourselves in the most picturesque village in Sikkim, Singla Bazaar, noted for its wide-spreading trees, well-laid-out huts, and variety of colours. When we arrived, the local policeman was paying his attentions to a native beauty. He should have come and saluted us on the spot, and then collected our pass. But we left Singla Bazaar with the document in our pockets, and it was not until we were some five or six miles from the village that we heard a shout, and saw a panting object behind us making frantic efforts to arrest our attention. Anqui interpreted for us on this occasion, and here is the translation from Sikkimese into English. Said the constable, "The great Sahib will gently say nothing to the mighty White Ruler of his country because a poor Sikkimese policeman loves his sweetheart and forgot to collect the paper on which are printed words granting permission to the Sahib to walk in the country of Sikkim."

Sikkim is a land of monasteries. The oldest and most famous of these unique institutions are Dubdi, Pamionchi, and Tashiding. Each of these is difficult of access. We wanted to visit all three—fate decided we should visit none. Our servant assured us that Tashiding monastery was inaccessible. This we doubted. What he really meant was that its situation involved a climb which perhaps was too fatiguing for the Sahib to undertake. The building is rather un-get-at-able save for holy men, whose progress to it is assisted by gods. Tashiding monastery stands upon the brink of a precipice—at least, it appeared so from our point of view. As the Lamas were expecting a visit from us, we sent excuses by one of their number who had thoughtfully come to conduct us to the place. We asked Anqui how he had translated our apologies into Tibetan, and his effort worked out something like this: "The powerful and learned Sahib of blessed fame sends his love to his black-hearted brothers of the Tashiding Monastery and asks to be forgiven for refusing to undertake the death journey up the precipice because he has no Shanks' pony to tie to his feet. His boots are worn out and there are holes in his socks, his feet want washing, too. May God help you!"

So we gave up Tashiding and turned our faces towards Pamionchi.

Pamionchi Monastery looks very imposing from a

distance. We asked Anqui to send a message to the Abbot advising that dignitary of our intention ot paying a State visit on the morrow. But Anqui looked glum, and muttered something about how difficult it would be for the Sahib to get within a mile of the building. However, the message was duly sent, and when the morrow came we were waited upon by a deputation of six Lamas, who kindly offered to escort us to the monastery. Anqui washed our feet before departing. He strongly urged us not to wear boots or shoes on the way to the holy of holies. We took his advice and had not proceeded half a mile before we were bitten by a grass snake. One of the accompanying Lamas took in the situation at a glance, as the novelists say, and flattened us on the ground as a professional boxer does his opponent. Before we knew what he was about, he had made a hole in our right foot about two inches square, and that with a dirty knife. Soon he was poulticing the wound with a substance he had plucked from the bush. Anqui said it was good, and that we should not die "just yet." Preparations were hastily made for our immediate return to the Dak Bungalow. A stretcher was improvised out of bamboo trees. Four of the Lamas acted as bearers, chanting their plaintive hymns that reminded us more of Chopin's Funeral March than songs of praise and thanks to the Lord Buddha for saving the life of the Sahib. Arrived at the Bungalow, hot water, soap and zinc ointment washed away whatever poison was in the wound. A few hours after we felt ourselves again. A present of twenty rupees to the kind Lamas and our mutual blessings, with a host of regrets to the Abbott of the monastery for our inability to be present with him in person, terminated the incident.

Pamionchi is nearly 7,000 feet above the level of the sea, and its monastery is the largest in Sikkim. The present building is practically new, and occupies the site of the one that was partially destroyed by fire some years ago. Unfortunately its roof is made of corrugated iron, and this eye-sore naturally spoils the appearance of the structure, so unlike anything Lamaist. On a bright, hot day, the roof can be seen shimmering many miles away. Speaking generally, the monastery possesses little dignity, either inside or out. As already remarked, it is situated in a part of the country where the most wonderful views of the Eastern Himalaya can be obtained, and the choice of its site speaks volumes for that keen perception of the sublime in Nature that characterises every devout Buddhist.

At certain seasons of the year, the Lamas of Pamionchi monastery go in groups to worship at the shrine of Mount Kanchenjunga, when Maha Kala, the Overlord of all the Spirits, is glorified. The ceremony entails a very strenuous journey, and is an exceedingly impressive one. It lasts for several days, and no objection is taken by the Lamas to the presence of Europeans among them. You are asked not to smoke during the ceremony.

As already mentioned, smoking is forbidden in Tibet by the Dalai Lama. But we found that the prohibition was not everywhere strictly observed, and the greatest offenders in this respect were the officials of the Tibetan Government. The Jong-pön of Phari, for example, once confiscated a consignment of tobacco from Bhutan, and was complimented by his Government for his "sagacity" in seizing and destroying the noxious weed, which appeared to have been imported into Phari as cow-dung, a commodity much in demand in this part of the world. But Dame Rumour has it that the Jong-pön appropriated the tobacco to himself, and its destruction was effected by his consuming the lot, with the aid of some English pipes presented to him by us on our way up country.

It was difficult for the majority of us to forego the luxury of tobacco while in Tibet, although we always did our best to conceal the habit from the authorities. We know we did not always succeed, and in consequence the Tibetans formed a rather indifferent opinion of us, generally speaking. Nor did we make much effort to convince the Tibetans of our devotion to Buddhism. Now and then Dr. McGovern, himself a Buddhist priest, would conduct a service in the Dak Bungalow, and invite the servants to participate in our supplications. But Dr. McGovern was not a very inspiring man in this connexion, although his voice must have reached the ears of the Dalai Lama enthroned in Lhasa, one hundred and fifty miles away. Doubtless we should have been more composed at these services had we once not detected Anqui putting his hands into the pockets of one of his fellows, and extracting coin of the realm from it. On another occasion, just behind the back of the bellowing high priest, and also during prayers, three of our boys began playing at dice to while away the time. The native schoolmaster at Gyantse, who spoke English rather well, and taught little Tibetan boys and girls to sing Tibetan songs to the tune of "Auld Lang Syne," "Mother McCree," "Molly McIntyre," etc., was always on the *qui-vive*, and his reports to the Tibetan officials on our conduct in general were not couched in very favourable terms. This, however, did not trouble us greatly, since we afterwards learned that he never thought well of anyone outside of his own race, and his opinions of Mr. MacDonald, the British Trade Agent, and Col. Bailey, the Political Officer, are unprintable. He was engaged to spy upon us during our month's stay in Gyantse, and he was candid enough to admit it while under the effects of a strong dose of Indian whisky, the worst in the world, which everyone is strictly forbidden to drink in Tibet, although all the Tibetan officials with whom we came in contact admired its flavour exceeding much. However, we fear that our attempts to adapt ourselves to the new conditions failed rather lamentably, although the majority of the members of our party were more or less abstainers, and comported themselves correctly.

Adventurous spirits who desire to visit Nepal without the sanction of the Nepalese Government will find their quest a difficult one. The fact is, Nepal is as "forbidden" a land as Tibet itself. Little is known of its interior. This country of 60,000 square miles is wedged in between India and the Kingdom of the Grand Lama. Its highest point lies in the neighbourhood of the icy regions of Mount Everest, from whence it slopes in a southerly direction to the plains of India. In consequence, it suffers extremes of climate. Its proximity to Darjeeling is such that we could not forego the luxury of being turned back by the frontier guards. At one time we thought that its inaccessible mountains would enable us to escape the vigilance of the Nepalese officials, but they seemed to be posted everywhere and in the least likely places.

Nepal is one of the most independent of the so-called Independent or Native States of India. Even to the native Indian, Nepal is a "foreign" country. That means that the British Raj is not at liberty to interfere with the internal affairs of the State. In Nepal there are neither British soldiers nor British police. The only link that binds Nepal with British India is that of the person of a British Political Officer or Consul. Like Tibet, Nepal wants to be left severely alone, to work out her own destiny, and be free from foreign influences.

The most striking feature about Nepal is its shape. No other country in the world can boast of possessing a piece of land, almost flat, situated in the middle of a vast system of mountains that contain the life and activities of the little State of some seven million souls. The site on which the capital of Nepal is situated was formerly a huge mountain lake, and the very hills now surrounding it were once lashed by its waters. It is now a well cultivated and populous valley, some 4,500 feet abouve the level of the sea, twenty miles long by fifteen broad.

In Katmandu, the capital, are to be found the creations of both ancient and modern civilisations—electric light, public baths, motor cars, gardens, temples, shrines and burning ghats. In addition to Katmandu, the Valley of Nepal, as it is called, contains the cities of Bhatagon and Patan and lesser places, as well as the famous burning ghat of Pashpatti. Eight languages are spoken by the inhabitants, of which the Gurkha, Newar, and Lepcha are the principal. Some of the Nepalese speak the *Parbattia Bhasa*, a Prakit or vulgar Sanskrit tongue.

Of archæological remains, Nepal will probably furnish the world with many surprises. Unfortunately, it is impossible to get the necessary permission of the Government to conduct archæological research in the country, all such requests being regarded with suspicion by the authorities, perhaps not without reason. Buddhist scholarship is deeply interested in Nepal. It is interesting to note in this connexion that not only did the Buddha travel in Nepal after his Enlightenment, but two hundred years later the great king Asoka journeyed to the valley, conquered the country, and established the capital of Patan, two miles to the south-east of the modern Katmandu. Here a number of monuments in the form of obelisks, etc., many containing the decrees of Asoka, were erected, as was also a temple which still stands near the palace of the present Maharajah. It is in districts that have been seldom or never yet visited by the White Man, that so much has to be brought to light. Perhaps one day the Nepalese Government will be induced to permit of archæological research being carried out in the country, under the eyes of their own officials if necessary.

It will suffice here to say that the two principal races in Nepal are the Gurkhas and the Newars. The Gurkhas are of Tibetan origin, but have become modified under different climatic, cultural and racial influences. Twelve branches of the Gurkhas are known, of which the Magars and Gurungs are the most famous, these being the two branches who enlist in Indian Gurkha regiments. They are of purer Bhotiya race and less completely Hinduized.

The Gurkhas are the ruling race of Nepal, having conquered the country in 1768. The religious system of the land is a compromise between Buddhism and Brahmanism. Like Sikkim, Tibet, and Bhutan, Nepal was never troubled with the great Mohammedan invasion of the twelfth and thirteenth centuries. Indeed, the onslaught on India by the Mohammedan hosts was virtually spent before it reached the Himalayan States.

The best way to reach the confines of Nepal from British Darjeeling is through Jorepokri, Tonglu, Sandakphu, Phalut, and Chiabanjan. This route lies along the eastern frontier of Nepal for nearly the whole distance. The march is uphill to Sandakphu, where the view of the snows is a never-to-be-forgotten one. Something of its grandeur may be faintly imagined when it is stated that the observer is confronted by two of the highest mountains in the world, Everest and Kanchenjunga. Apart from the snowy whiteness around, there are many other interesting sights to be seen, including deep and gloomy valleys, gorges, forests of every variety and description, and, if one is lucky enough at certain seasons of the year, of numerous rhododendron copses.

Our destination was Chiabanjan, or " The hollow where one looks over from Nepal " into Sikkim. We chose this spot because we had been informed of the presence there of Nepalese guards who would turn their heads in any direction we desired at the sight of a few rupees. We stayed the night in a very tumbledown native house infested with leeches. Some of these duly attacked us, but the application of salt to the pests invariably put an end to their existence. At one time our new servant had to apply sodium of chloride to the bodies of no less than nineteen leeches which had attached themselves to our legs. After that we were troubled by mosquitoes. There was no mosquito curtain to hand when it was wanted—our boy had " mislaid " it, at least, that is what he told us. But we got to learn that he had " borrowed " it for wrapping purposes. The child of a native woman, it appeared, had died from an attack of small pox, and the mother needed something to wrap the corpse in. The mosquito curtain being the handiest and nearest article at our most sympathetic servant's disposal, was promptly seized upon as a shroud. It was returned in due course, unwashed, with the explanation that " Leetle baby die clean death —mosquitoes soon die now."

Which reminds us that a few days previous to this incident, our cook had served up some most delicious " Jugged hare." We were curious to know how he came into possession of a hare! " O, Sạh," was the answer we received, " me saw big snake eat little jackal. Me kill snake, and then take little jackal from snake's belly."

A twenty-rupee present enabled us to romp in Nepalese territory for three days. The guide kept us from native villages in order to avoid suspicion, and as we were under contract not to go anywhere without him, and he kept his eyes on our provisions, etc., our excursion to Nepal did not prove a very exciting affair after all.

THE BUDDHISM OF TIBET.*

* See *What is Buddhism? an answer from the Western point of view.* Price 3s. 6d. The Buddhist Lodge, London.

The founder of Buddhism was Siddharta Gautama, or Gotama, who later became known as Sakya Muni, "Sage of the Sakyas," and Tathagata, "he who has attained the goal (Nirvana)." He was born between 600 B.C., at Kapilavastu, in the modern Nepal. He was an original thinker and teacher, profoundly impressed with the struggle of Life and its associated problems of Sorrow and Suffering. The major portion of his long life was devoted to the spiritual uplift of his fellow men, to a discovery of a means of escaping from the Wheel of Life, of attaining a condition of mind and heart commonly known as Nirvana. The son of King Suddhodana, who ruled over the Sakya tribes, he married, when quite young, the Princess Yasodara, by whom he had a son, Rahula.

It is commonly said that his horoscope at birth foretold his high destiny, that he would become one of the world's greatest teachers, and not remain content with regal surroundings. He had not been married very long when the object of his life was revealed to him, and "The Great Renunciation" followed soon after his realisation that Life was obviously involved with Suffering. "Birth is suffering, decay is suffering, disease is suffering, separation from the pleasant is suffering, and every craving that remains unsatisfied is suffering."

While all is suffering, everything is impermanent—life, riches, glory, honour, hope, despair, have their day and are gone. No one thing is the same at this moment as it was a moment ago. The sun, the moon, the sidereal universe, each and all have changed since these lines were written a moment ago. "Change and decay in all around I see," says Christian. The poet, Shelley, put it in this way: "Naught may endure but Mutability." "The paths of glory," wrote Gray, "lead but to the grave." And Shakespeare: "Impermanent are all component things."

Suffering, in the Buddhist sense, not only includes everything that we usually associate with pain and disease, but also with such feelings as discord, friction, irritation, discomfort, etc. Suffering is common throughout the physical universe—only Nature's enlightened few escape its pangs.

Gotama, the Buddha, became an ascetic in order to find a means of escape from this Wheel of Suffering, and to teach it, when found, to his fellow-men. For some time after leaving wife and child, father and mother, home and wealth, he associated with hermits and ascetics of all sorts in an effort to find an answer to his question, carefully examining and putting to a test the numerous theories of emancipation that were taught him. But in none of these could he find satisfaction, and eventually he abandoned the ascetic's life, realising that wisdom and salvation are to be found within one's own self alone, and not in austerities and penance. So he put aside asceticism as detrimental to the physical and spiritual welfare of man, and retired alone into the forests to find his own heart's peace and understanding.

It was while he was sitting under the Tree of Wisdom, or the Bodhi Tree, as it is called, that he attained Enlightenment, and for forty-five years thereafter he wandered over Northern India, spreading the message of "Salvation by Self-Effort." For Buddhism, be it noted, is essentially a philosophy of individual effort; according to the Buddhist, there is nothing in the world, or out of it, to save humanity but humanity's own self.

Buddhism, therefore, teaches self-reliance, self-control, self-culture, self-development, self-respect.

With the founding of the Buddhist *Sangha*, an Order of all those who had renounced the world to attain deliverance, monks were sent to different parts of Asia to teach the Law. In this manner, Buddhism came to be disseminated throughout India, Ceylon, and Burma. Four hundred years after the death of the Buddha, the doctrine had established itself in practically the whole of Asia, and is now embraced by nearly one-third of the human race. For reasons which cannot be gone into now, Buddhism has been practically extinct in India since the Mohammedan invasion of the sub-continent in the twelfth century, and it is only in such places as Burma, Siam, and Ceylon that primitive Buddhism is to be found to-day. Buddhism did not reach Tibet until the seventh century of the Christian era, after it had suffered considerable corruption in the land of its birth. Tibet, in fact, was the last of the Southern Mongol countries to receive its Buddhism.

It was the result of a war that brought Buddhism to Tibet, a war between that country and its powerful eastern neighbour, China. One of the conditions of peace of this conflict was the giving of a Chinese princess in marriage to the then reigning king of Tibet, who had already married a Nepalese woman. As both of these women were Buddhists, they took upon themselves the task of converting the King to their religion. But King Srong-stan Gam-po, as he was called, seems to have been more of a warrior than a man devoted to lofty moral ideals, and even after his alleged conversion to Buddhism, he continued to make war on neighbouring states. However, he did his best to make the Buddhism of his day the state religion of the country over which he ruled. That he did not achieve much success was due to the fact that at that time Tibet was sunk in barbarism and ignorance. There is little doubt that cannibalism was then rife in Tibet. It was reserved for the King's son, in association with a very famous Indian Guru, to establish the new religion in Tibet, or rather to lay the foundations of the new religion. Naturally, many years of opposition from the priests of the Bön, or indigenous religion of the country, had to be overcome before any real progress could be made. And it was not Buddhism that became the state religion of Tibet, but a very elaborate system of metaphysics and demonology, in which deities of Brahmanic origin, such as Indra, Vishnu, and Brahma were incorporated, while parts of the pre-Buddhist religion of Tibet also found a place. The present religious system of Tibet may be said to be a hotch-potch of Hinduism, Buddhism, and Metaphysics, plus a code of beliefs that prevailed in the country before the much-corrupted form of Buddhism was introduced. Tibetan Lamaism, or priestcraft, resolves itself into a system of religious monopoly not unlike that which prevailed in Europe before the Reformation.

Long before the advent of Lamaism, Buddhism had become metaphysical and ritualistic in India and elsewhere. A permanent schism was established in the first century of our era into the "Northern" and "Southern" Schools, the Mahayana and Hinayana respectively, or the "Greater and Lesser Vehicles," as they have come to be called. Whereas primitive Buddhism was devoid of dogmas to be accepted on blind faith, and knew nothing of ceremonies conducive to salvation, nor of a creator to whom worship was to be made, nor yet of a soul to be saved, the Mahayana School of Buddhism which found its way into Tibet was essentially theistic. In consequence of the deification of the founder of Buddhism, it had by then become an actual religion as distinct from a philosophy. The adoration of the Buddha's relics, the cult instituted in his honour, the introduction of mystical teachings, all naturally tended to degrade the original doctrine. Rather than as apostles of the Buddha, the Lamas of Tibet may be regarded, in the main, as exorcists and magicians.

The Lama is a priest invested by ordination. And not only is he a priest. He is educator, teacher, doctor, astrologer, sorcerer, architect, painter, plumber, and printer, to say nothing of being a merchant. He is not compelled to take the vow of poverty and he generally possesses a considerable fortune.

The consequence of the rather depressing system of Lamaism is that science, literature, and art, as we Westerners understand these terms, are almost unknown in Tibet. The few colleges that exist in the neighbourhood of Shigatse, Gyantse, and Lhasa are devoted almost exclusively to the study of the religious beliefs of the land, with reading, writing and arithmetic. The learning consists of the Tangyur and Kangyur, the two collections of the sacred canon of Tibetan Buddhism, believed by Western scholars to contain much that is unknown of the early history and philosophy of India. There are also the Tantric books, and the works of the famous Tibetan ascetic-poet, Milarepa, and the Tibetan Book of the Dead. These two latter volumes have only recently been translated into English, each a monumental work in itself, giving a new insight into the religious system of the country as a whole. Nothing is printed in the Hermit Kingdom without the permission of those in authority, nor can it well be, since all the printing presses are in the possession of the monasteries. The existing social system of Tibet being based on a theocracy, open expression of opinion is unknown. The suspicions of the Tibetans, their aversion from the foreigners, are due to their fear of invasion and the exploitation of their country by foreign capitalists. Secret societies exist in Tibet for the purpose of keeping the foreigner out, to prevent innovations, to get rid of the Dalai Lama, and to substitute "Red" for "Yellow" rule. Every monastery throughout the country has its secret society, and it may even happen that one monastery has two or three such institutions, each working against the other, either to secure the government of the monastery, or a change in its organisation. One monastery occasionally wages war with another, the combatants, for the most part, being the roughest elements specially retained for this purpose. These are the famous "fighting" monks, or hooligans of Tibet.

* * *

One of the most important differences between

organised, official Christianity and primitive Buddhism is the doctrine of Resurrection on the one hand, and of Re-incarnation (Re-birth) on the other. Christianity rejects Re-incarnation absolutely, although it was formerly accepted and taught as a cardinal doctrine of faith, but to-day is held by the sect of Christian Gnostics alone among Christians. Many of the most illustrious fathers of the Christian Church believed in Re-incarnation before it was condemned as anathema. To-day it is accepted by a very large number of the leading men and women of the Western world. Re-incarnation is the central doctrine of the Buddhist religion. Christianity recognises but one universe, the present, and two lives, the natural or physical body, and the one to come in that of Resurrection. Christianity therefore not only puts a very definite limit to the number of man's earthly lives, but goes farther. According to the Christian point of view, everything that a man now does determines whether he is to live for ever in a state of bliss, or is to perish miserably in an everlasting hell fire.

Not so with Buddhism. To the Buddhist there are a countless series of universes, which have come into being during a countless series of eternities, and being impermanent, will pass away to give birth to yet others. Modern Astronomy appears to support this view of things. To the Buddhist, a man reaps what he has sown, and nothing else. The Buddhist believes that he will experience an almost infinite number of Re-births until at last he will be liberated from the cycle of birth and death, and will then attain freedom in Nirvana. The Buddhist claims that no outside power can destroy the fruit of a man's good and evil actions. Says the *Dhammapada*: " By oneself the evil is done; by oneself one is purified." Nor can he escape the consequences of his actions: " Not in the sky, not in the midst of the sea, nor anywhere else on earth is there a spot where a man may be freed from the consequences of an evil deed." But that which is done can by the doer be in due time undone. This is contingent on the deeds now being done. A man to-day is but the product of his past actions, the *Karma* he has inherited. Karma means *action, doing, deed,* and is a universal, all-embracing law, by his knowledge of which a man moulds his future. Primitive Buddhism urges that a belief in the supernatural is detrimental to the individual, that it destroys self-reliance, self-confidence, self-respect, etc.

But the emotional, deeply religious demon-ridden people of Tibet find in their curious blend of Buddhism, Hinduism, Metaphysics, etc., all that is satisfying to their needs. To make their religious system a comprehensive and workable whole, certain deities had to be introduced who, it was claimed, would lend a sympathetic ear to those in need. The Gods of Contemplation, five in all, were thereupon embodied in the religious system of the country, of which Chenraisi, the most important of the quintette, is incarnate in the Dalai Lama. In consequence of the doctrine held by all devout Tibetans, the Dalai Lamas of Tibet and the other incarnated Lamas never die. When the physical body is worn out by sickness or old age, the god, whose spirit animates it, leaves the body to seek for another in good health. In other words, it becomes incarnate in some young infant who reveals his divine nature to those whose business it is to seek it out.

Chenraisi, the Tibetan form of Avalokita, or Avalokite-svara, " the Keen Seeing Lord, the Great Pitier and Lord of Mercy," is the spiritual son of the celestial Buddha Amitabha, and the most popular and powerful of all the Bodhisats. Being a purely mythological personage, he has assumed several forms of a supernatural nature. Avalokita is of Indian origin, and his earliest image shows him in the form of the Hindu creator, Brahma. It was Avalokita who took pity upon the offspring of the monkey and she-devil by giving them a magic grain which had the effect of converting the unhappy youngsters into human beings when they were found by the god wandering in the high Himalaya. The Tibetans believe in the animal origin of their race.

The images inside every monastery in Tibet are interesting. Many of them are well made, though the majority of the paintings would not be tolerated in any civilised country. Of the former, the historical Buddha is only to be found occasionally, as the Lamas prefer to make obeisance at the shrine of the non-human Buddhas, of whom Maitreya is the principal. Maitreya, known as the Compassionate One, is believed by all Tibetian schools of Buddhism to be the coming Buddha. Maitreya is often shown with Caucasian features, and this has given rise to the belief that the Buddhist Messiah will enter Asia from the west. Of the paintings seen by us, not a few of them are of the type commonly known in the west as "Postures of Matrimony." Sexually, the Tibetans adopt a rather primitive standard. When it has been discovered that a man has had illicit relations with the wife of another man, the guilty party generally makes amends by going in person to the aggrieved husband, and apologising for his offence. A reconciliation is effected by the offer of a *khatag*, or scarf, with an intimation that the wife of the guilty party will receive the injured husband at his convenience

The Tibetian Lamas claim not only to be able to "regulate" a person's karma, but to be able to postpone re-birth. One very interesting of such cases came our way in Phari. A well-to-do merchant had grown tired both of living and dying. By the simple expedient of turning a prayer wheel containing the mystic charm of Chenraisi, *Om! ma-ni pad-me Hum!* and endowing the Chatsa monastery with money, he was spared the pain of living a thousand lives and dying a thousand deaths by a re-incarnated Lama who enjoyed a privileged acquaintance with one of the numerous gods that prey upon the imagination of the devil-ridden Tibetans.

Throughout Tibet, and extending into Sikkim, Bhutan, Kashmir, Nepal, and even to parts of Mongolia, there are to be found three principal Schools of Lamaism. The first is the "Middle Way," the second the "Great Symbol," and the third the "Great Perfection." To Westerners the first School is better known as the sect of the Yellow Caps, or "Followers of the Virtuous Order." This School was founded at the beginning of the fifteenth century, and is called the Ge-lug-pas. His

Holiness the Dalai Lama is at the head of this Reformed Church. The adherents of "The Great Symbol" are known as the Karg-ut-pas, or "Followers of the Apostolic Succession," of which Milarepa, the poet-ascetic of Tibet, is considered the greatest of the Tibetan Apostles. The followers of the "Great Perfection," or "The Old Style Ones," are commonly known as Red Caps, or the adherents of the Unreformed Church. They are popularly regarded by the Western world as the retrogrades of Tibet, who dislike innovations and desire the country to remain free of Western civilisation.

In addition, there are monastic orders which still survive beneath each of the above Schools. In the central and eastern portions of the country, particularly in the U and Tsang provinces, the pre-Lamaist religion of the country, the Bön or Bön-pa, persists to a very large extent side by side with the three national Schools, from which it has borrowed many of their customs. From the colour of the robes worn by the priests of this sect, it is known as the "Blacks," to distinguish it from the orthodox "Yellow" and dissenting "Reds." In this religion there are eighteen principal deities, the most famous being the red and black demons, the snake devil, and the fiery tiger god, pictures and statues of which were shown to us on our visit to Gyantse monastery. In many of the mystery plays of Tibet, as well as in the so-called "Devil" dances, images of these gods of the old Bön religion of the country are employed.